High Altitude Attitudes

High Altitude Attitudes
Six Savvy Colorado Women

Marilyn Griggs Riley

Foreword by Thomas J. Noel

Johnson Books, Boulder

Published by Johnson Books, a division of Big Earth Publishing,
3005 Center Green Drive, Suite 220, Boulder, Colorado 80301.
E-mail: books@bigearthpublishing.com
www.johnsonbooks.com

Cover design by Polly Christensen
Cover photos: Western History Department, Denver Public Library
Text design and composition by D. Kari Luraas, Clairvoyance Design

9   8   7   6   5   4   3   2   1

Library of Congress Cataloging-in-Publication Data
Riley, Marilyn Griggs.
   High altitude attitudes: six savvy Colorado women/Marilyn Griggs Riley
      p. cm.
   ISBN 1-55566-375-3
1. Women—Colorado—Biography. 2. Women—Colorado—History. 3. Colorado—History—19th century. 4. Colorado—History—20th century. 5. Colorado—Biography. I. Title.
   CT23260.R55 2006
   978.8'0330922—dc22
                                                    2006005661

Printed in the United States of America

To the best teachers—
especially Dudley R. Griggs, Jr.,
Conrad M. Riley, MD,
Anne, Burke, and Robb Griggs

Contents

Foreword
by Thomas J. Noel

Marilyn Hughes Griggs Riley has taught, written, and promoted literature for the last thirty years. She is a writer and intimate of such literary celebrities as Colorado's late, great poet laureate, about whom she wrote the Emmy Award–winning PBS documentary *Thomas Hornsby Ferril: One Mile Five-Foot Ten*. Riley knew some of the characters showcased in this delightful anthology. Using interviews, letters, articles, and other sources, she exhumes from their tombs six amazing spirits.

Although Colorado began with twenty men for each woman, according to the first (1860) census, the women soon caught up. In 1893 the ladies persuaded men to make Colorado the first state where males voted for women's suffrage. (Suffrage was only one part of a large constitutional package approved earlier by the men of Wyoming.)

Armed with the vote, women began making a difference, advancing art, drama, education, health, literature, medicine, religion, and public welfare. Sadly, some of Colorado's most accomplished women are largely forgotten today. In this book Riley brings back to life six wonderful characters who should not be forgotten. She deliberately picked six women about whom a book has never been written.

My favorite is the first Coloradan ever to win a Pulitzer Prize and, arguably, Colorado's leading literary luminary. Mary Coyle Chase was a bright, imaginative, bold Irish girl whose childhood home, a humble cottage at 532 West Fourth Avenue, is now a designated Denver Landmark. Riley provides the most detailed profile available of a woman who deserves a book. Chase grew up in a poor Irish family haunted by leprechauns and pookas (giant animals similar to Harvey, the six-foot-one-and-a-half-inch white rabbit of Chase's Pulitzer-winning play). Riley, who knew Chase as a fellow member of the Denver Woman's Press Club, describes her as "a beautiful woman with a flawless complexion and luxuriant brown hair swept back from her face."

Chase's derring-do as a reporter trampled over the tightly proscribed boundaries of a woman's role. She sneaked into mines, into the Denver Country Club, and into Denver General Hospital to interview an old Chinaman dying penniless far from his native land.

After personally struggling with a drinking problem, Chase founded the Hope House for female alcoholics. She stood in labor picket lines and wrote and spoke out for oppressed working people, including the Hispanics toiling at the low end of Colorado's pecking order. Like Molly Brown, Mary Coyle Chase rose from near the bottom to the top of Denver's social circles, winding up in a mansion at 505 Circle Drive.

Riley, a highly respected and much-loved English teacher at Denver's Manual High School for twenty years, analyzes the plays as well as their writer. She concludes that Mary Coyle Chase, who believed in the healing power of laughter, got the last laugh. Chase lies in Lakewood's Crown Hill Cemetery next to a stone inscribed "Harvey."

Besides Mary Coyle Chase, Riley focuses on Louise Sneed Hill, who topped Denver society along with the Bonfils sisters, squabbling heiresses of the *Denver Post* millions. Riley compassionately but objectively profiles her longtime friend, the best-selling writer Caroline Bancroft, who is still controversial for her sometimes fictionalized histories of leading Colorado characters.

Riley also includes hard-found facts on the legendary, little-known African black physician Dr. Justina Ford. "You have two strikes against you," she was told when applying to practice medicine in Colorado. "First off, you're a lady, and second, you're colored."

Marilyn Griggs Riley does a splendid job in these fascinating pages of sharing her long-standing, highly original work on six leading ladies in the Highest State. You, dear reader, are in for a treat as you meet these women with high-altitude attitudes that make them enduring role models.

Acknowledgments

This history is possible only through the efforts of all the people cited elsewhere—those who generously contributed their valuable time for interviews—and scores of others who helped at every step of the research and writing process. Those faithful friends include editor Joan White, Virginia McGehee, JoAnn Hamling, Vanessa Martin, and Linda Wiggs.

Members of the Denver Public Library's priceless resource, the Western History Department, provided immense help and patience: Judy Brown, David Bustamente, Coi Drummond-Gehrig, Bruce Hanson, Joan Harms, John Irwin, James Jeffrey, Jim Kroll, Marty Lister, Colleen Nunn, Phil Panum, Janice Prater, Trina Purcell, and Kay Wisnia.

The Colorado Historical Society's David N. Wetzel, publications editor, and Steve Grinstead, editor of *Colorado Heritage*, were helpful and extraordinary models of scholarship.

Thanks also to Sandra Dallas, James and Barbara Hartley, Joyce B. Lohse, Wallace Yvonne Tollette, and to the Black American West Museum and Heritage Center that shared their photographs.

Timeline

1858	William G. Russell party, from Auraria, Georgia, discovers gold near the South Platte River. Auraria and Denver are founded. Cottonwoods and willows are the only trees native to the area.
1859	Tens of thousands join in the Pikes Peak Gold Rush.
1861	Colorado Territory is carved from Kansas Territory. US President Lincoln appoints William Gilpin the first territorial governor.
1870	Denver population: 4,759; Colorado's population: 39,864. Denver Pacific and Kansas Pacific railroads connect Denver to the national rail network, ending its isolation and stagnation.
1876	Colorado becomes thirty-eighth state on August 1.
1877	University of Colorado opens with forty-four students.
1878	Central City, the "richest square mile on earth," and the most important gold mining town in the Rocky Mountains, builds an opera house financed by 15,000 residents.
1879	Horace A. W. Tabor buys Henry C. Brown mansion on a block of ground bordered by Broadway and Lincoln Streets at Seventeenth Avenue. Agricultural College of Colorado (later CSU) opens in Fort Collins.
1880	Denver population: 35,629; Colorado population: 194,327. Electricity powers Denver. Ute Indian chief Ouray dies. State Normal College (later UNC) opens in Greeley.
1881	Grand Junction is founded. Tabor Grand Opera House opens on Sixteenth Street between Arapahoe and Curtis. Denver builds Arapahoe County Courthouse at Fourteenth and Larimer Streets.
1882	First steel is milled in Pueblo.

1886	Denver Union Stockyards are established and cattle are unloaded at Union Station, and herded east to Downing Street and north to stockyards.
	Fire ordinances restrict Denver buildings to masonry/brick construction.
1890	Denver population:106,713; Colorado population: 413,249.
	Cornerstone of State Capitol laid. Grant Street, the heart of Capitol Hill, is nicknamed "Millionaire's Row."
	Sherman Silver Purchase Act raises price of silver to more than $1 per ounce.
	Denver has 300 saloons.
	Elitch Zoological Gardens and Elitch Theater open.
1892	Downtown Denver's Brown Palace Hotel and Equitable Building open.
	First streets are topped with asphalt.
1893	Colorado is the second state (after Wyoming) to extend suffrage to women.
	Sherman Silver Act is repealed; Silver Crash and economic depression result.
	State's boom-and-bust economic cycle begins.
1900	Denver population: 133,859; Colorado population: 539,700.
	State's urban population is 48.3 percent.
	Women are 22 percent of state workforce: teachers, dressmakers, servants, saleswomen, waitresses, stenographers, doctors, and lawyers.
	Denver has 4,500 telephones.
1900–1920	Nearly $500 million worth of gold, mostly from Cripple Creek, pours in from Colorado mines.
1901	US president William McKinley is assassinated and Theodore Roosevelt succeeds him.
1902	Denver becomes "home rule" city and county carved from Adams and Arapahoe Counties.
	New Denver Public School District 1 has four high schools: North, East, West, and Manual Training.
1903	Jewish Consumptive Relief Society (JCRS) for tuberculosis patients is organized in Lakewood.

	Orville Wright flies an airplane at Kitty Hawk, North Carolina.
1904–1918	Mayor Robert W. Speer transforms Denver into a "City Beautiful."
	Civic Center and Speer Boulevard are graceful part of the renovation.
	Free elm and maple saplings are given to residents for seven years to shade Denver streets.
1905	Evangelical Lutheran Sanitarium, for care of tuberculars, is established in Wheat Ridge.
	Average wage in the US is $.22 per hour.
	Einstein's Theory of Relativity is published.
1906	"Welcome" and "Mizpah" decorate large iron Welcome Arch installed at Fifteenth and Wynkoop Streets in front of Union Station.
	Mesa Verde becomes national park.
1908	National Swedish Hospital is formed for tubercular patients in Englewood.
	Ford Motor Company introduces Model T.
1909	Craig Hospital in Edgewater is organized to aid tuberculars.
1910	Denver population: 213,381; Colorado population: 799,204.
	The Wonderful Wizard of Oz is published.
1911	Daniels & Fisher department store in downtown Denver adds a tower, built in image of Campanile of St. Mark's Square in Venice, and becomes city's tallest structure.
1912	Denver voters approve mountain parks amendment providing series of mountain parks and roads, designed with help of Frederick L. Olmsted, Jr., renowned landscape architect. Two mountain parks, Winter Park Ski Area and Red Rocks Amphitheater, later become tourist meccas.
	Agnes C. Phipps Sanitarium for tubercular patients is built and later absorbed by Lowry Air Force Base.
1913	Sixteenth Amendment to US Constitution authorizes federal income tax.
1914	World War I begins.

Panama Canal is completed.

Bethesda Hospital opens to serve tubercular patients.

1915   Rocky Mountain National Park is established.

1916   Emily Griffith Opportunity School is founded by Denver Public Schools.

Colorado votes for statewide prohibition of alcohol.

1917   US enters World War I.

1918   Fitzsimons Army Hospital, named for William Fitzsimons, first American medical officer to die in World War I, treats veterans with respiratory diseases incurred from trench warfare gassing.

1919   Pandemic flu claims 20 million lives worldwide.

Eighteenth Amendment to US Constitution enacts Prohibition.

1920   Denver population: 256,491; Colorado population: 939,629.

Ku Klux Klan comes to power with election of Klansmen Clarence Morley as governor and Ben Stapleton as mayor of Denver.

KLZ becomes Denver's first licensed radio station.

Agriculture replaces Colorado mining as state's top revenue producer.

Nineteenth Amendment to US Constitution gives women right to vote.

Chanel No. 5 perfume is created by French designer Coco Chanel, who also liberates women from corsets and designs new fashions that expose the ankle.

1925   Architect Temple H. Buell buys a fifty-five-acre city dump at First Avenue and University Boulevard, which he later develops into Cherry Creek Shopping Center.

1927   Charles Lindbergh is first to fly solo across Atlantic Ocean.

The Jazz Singer debuts as first "talkie" movie.

1928   Moffat Tunnel under the Continental Divide, links Denver railroads to Pacific Coast and augments city's water supply.

Mickey Mouse makes his first appearance in *Steamboat Willie*.

1929	Denver Municipal (Stapleton) Airport opens.
	Stock market crash on Wall Street; Great Depression begins.
1930	Denver population: 287,861; Colorado population: 1,035,791.
	Federal New Deal programs begin, including Works Progess Administration, Civilian Conservation Corps, and Public Works Administration.
1931	Total of 2,294 American banks fail.
	Denver City and County Building is erected.
1932	Central City Opera House reopens after extensive renovation.
	Five-year drought on eastern plains begins; dust storms suffocate crops and darken Rocky Mountain region in daytime.
1933	One of every four Coloradans is out of work.
	Castlewood Dam, thirty-two miles southeast of Denver, breaks; floodwaters spread to city's Twenty-Third Street viaduct. Later, Cherry Creek Dam is built to protect the area.
	Prohibition Amendment is canceled.
1934	Denver Symphony Orchestra is formed.
1935	Social Security Act is passed by US Congress.
1937	Denver is linked to nation by direct transcontinental air traffic routes.
	Lowry Air Force Base is named for Denver pilot Francis B. Lowry, shot down over France in World War I.
1940	Denver population: 322,412; Colorado population: 1,123,296.
	Allen True paints murals in state capitol rotunda; inscribed beneath panels is Thomas Hornsby Ferril's poem "Here is a land where life is written in water."
	Fitzsimons Army Hospital, refurbished and expanded, is largest structure in Colorado.
	Aurora becomes state's most populous bedroom community.
1941	Red Rocks amphitheater is dedicated.
	Japan bombs Pearl Harbor; US enters World War II.

	First US television program is broadcast.
1942	Rocky Mountain Arsenal is established to make lethal gases and napalm bombs.
	Amache internment camp for US citizens of Japanese-American descent is built in southeastern Colorado.
1945	World War II ends.
	New York City land developer William Zeckendorf describes Denver as "too spread out to be quaint and too ugly to be pleasant."
1947	Quigg Newton elected Denver mayor, reshapes municipal government: Denver's garbage collection contract with hog farmers is canceled and alleys are paved.
	Florence Sabin, MD, age seventy three, directs Denver's health department, launching X-ray program to diagnose tuberculosis. TB death rate drops 50 percent.
1948	US Supreme Court decision prohibits restrictive property covenants, ending local and national ethnic and racial segregation.
1949	*Rocky Mountain News* editorial describes Denver as "smug, satisfied, abhorrent of risk-taking, chary of progress."
1950	Denver population: 415,786; Colorado population: 1,325,089.
	Old Guard city leaders concede to new money, corporations, and conglomerates.
	Korean War begins.
1950–1960	New downtown buildings, like Mile High Center and Denver Club Building, exceed height of D&F Tower. Denver motor vehicle registration doubles over previous decade.
	Buses replace overhead electric trolleys that linked every part of Denver to suburbs, work, church, cemeteries, and mountain parks.
1951	Newton administration and City Council repeal Denver's 1908 twelve-story height limitation.
1952	Denver-Boulder Turnpike opens.
1953	Rocky Flats industrial complex, built by Atomic Energy Commission, opens.

1958	I-25, Denver's first official interstate highway, opens.
1960	Denver population: 493,887; Colorado population: 1,753,947.
	One-way streets are inaugurated by Denver traffic engineer Henry Barnes; "Barnes Dance" befuddles pedestrians, who now control intersections on walk traffic signal.
1966	I-70 interstate highway opens.
	Suburban populations boom as Denver's growth slows.
1969	Federal District Judge William Doyle orders racial desegregation in Denver Public Schools.
1970	Denver population: 514,678; Colorado population: 2,207,000.
	State's urban population approaches 80 percent.

Introduction

You go in high gear to Colorado, where fifty-four mountain peaks over 14,000 feet make it the highest state in the Union. Persistent land-rise from east to west strains horses, cars, and people. On the last crest you finally see the entire Rocky Mountain Front Range, its snowcapped peaks spanning the horizon. Perhaps right here, you think, is the place, that magical, unmarked spot where the West really begins! High altitude could be blamed for such irrational exuberance.

In 1859, miners, farmers, and their unsung wives were also dazzled—by gold fever or by the impossible dream of a western Eden longing to be plowed. Pioneers staked claims on the land, displacing the Arapaho, Cheyenne, and Ute. When the reality of few gold bonanzas and high plains drought trumped hope, the disillusioned abandoned their dreams and moved on. Still, thousands more kept coming. Isolated western outposts grew into towns, and seventeen years after the first rush to the Rockies, Colorado joined the Union. Females quickly began a campaign for equal suffrage, and in 1893, white male voters gave women the right to vote. They continued their efforts to raise the region's quality of life.

At the turn of the twentieth century, talented and competent Colorado females held an advantage over those in stable, older American cities with traditional, patriarchal values. Women in this isolated western, sparsely populated town invaded various male citadels where the mortar was barely dry. Denver's economic boom-and-bust pattern had caused broad social instability mitigated in part by the employment of women in venues that were unavailable to them elsewhere. Here, talent became more important than gender.

This book is about six women whose substantial achievements between 1900 and 1970 are mostly unappreciated by comparison with their famous contemporaries whose names made national headlines. Selecting these relatively unknown six was not a random process. Those who survived the painful winnowing process represent thousands of other vigorous, visionary women who did not.

One of those excluded is Anne Evans (1871–1941), daughter of the second territorial governor, John Evans. She was a founding member of the Denver Art Museum, the Central City Opera House

1

Association, and served on the Denver Public Library Commission for thirty years. Denver Symphony Orchestra founder Helen Black (1896–1988), the city's undisputed grande dame of the arts, is also absent. So are Mary Rippon (1850–1935), the University of Colorado's first female professor, and Emily Griffith (1868–1947), founder of her hugely successful Opportunity School. Another is Florence Sabin, MD (1871–1953), whose statue in the nation's Capitol honors her; she became the first woman professor at Johns Hopkins Medical School and the first woman member of the National Academy of Sciences, and the Rockefeller Institute for Medical Research named her the leading woman scientist in the world. After retirement, Dr. Sabin returned home where she angrily stopped the dumping of raw sewage into rivers and then revolutionized Denver's public health department.

Families of these women and unnamed others came west by oxcart, wagon, and railroad, modeling a strong work ethic their adult children emulated. Second- and third generation daughters worked in nearly every area of Colorado commerce, public health, law, the arts, education, charitable causes, and beautification. For example, Jane Silverstein Ries (1909–2005) was our first woman landscape artist. She quietly transformed Denver's limited palette of wide, open lawns and beds of predictable petunias to plant new materials in alkaline soil and arid conditions. Gladys Caldwell Fisher (1907–1952) chiseled many stone sculptures, including the two magnificent mountain sheep that guard the south portals of the federal courthouse on Eighteenth Street. Mary (Mrs. Verner Z.) Reed (1875–1945), nicknamed "Lady Bountiful" for her steady financial support to her city during the Great Depression, consistently financed University of Denver building construction, Community Chest/United Way, and the Civic Theater. Agnes Reid Tammen (1865–1942), the childless widow of Harry H. Tammen who cofounded the *Denver Post*, dedicated much of her energy and fortune to Children's Hospital.

Those women and their contemporaries shopped on downtown's Sixteenth Street at Daniels & Fisher; Gano-Downs, with its concave glass display windows; Neusteter's, at Stout Street across from Gano-Downs; the Denver Dry Goods Co., at California Street; Fontius Shoe Co.; Fashion Bar; Three Sisters; and off Sixteenth Street, the elegant Montaldo's. Ladies lunched on crabcakes at the Denver Dry

Tea Room, ordered ice cream sodas at Bauer's Restaurant on Curtis Street, and occasionally sneaked into the basement cafeteria at the Champa Street Woolworth's, the largest five-and-dime store west of the Mississippi River. Sixteenth Street was the best—and only—place to go. Before 1953, there were no shopping centers or fast-food chains. Restaurants and stores were closed on Sundays.

The six women portrayed here significantly impacted Denver and Colorado between 1900 and 1970. Their high-profile contemporaries were Margaret (Molly) Brown (1867–1932) of *Titanic* fame; the rags-to-riches-to-rags Baby Doe Tabor (1854–1935); Mary Elitch Long (1856–1936) of Elitch Gardens; Mamie Doud Eisenhower (1896–1979), the nation's popular first lady; and Golda Meir (1898–1978), who became the fourth prime minister of Israel.

Profiled here are Louise Sneed Hill, Justina Ford, MD, May Bonfils Stanton, Helen G. Bonfils, Caroline Bancroft, and Mary Coyle Chase. Most of these lively women knew one another. During the first seventy years of the twentieth century, Denver grew from a small, dusty town of 134,000 residents on the edge of the Great American Desert to a sprawling metropolitan area with paved streets and urban congestion.

Louise Hill was a visiting southern belle who met and married Denver's wealthiest bachelor, lived in a sumptuous mansion, and made society her career. Women of her wealth and era had few career options. However, her broad network of famous people in important places, her charm, her strategies, and managerial skills applied a century later could have taken her to the highest level of corporate success. Instead Louise wrote Denver's social register, which is still published annually.

Justina Ford, like Louise Hill, moved from the South to Denver. In fact the two women lived within three miles of each other, although they never met. In their time America was a racially segregated nation and Justina, the first black woman physician in Colorado, lived and practiced in Five Points. She delivered more than 7,000 babies in their homes during her fifty-year medical practice. After decades of applying for membership in national and local medical associations, she was finally accepted and only then awarded standard hospital privileges.

May Bonfils, the elder, feisty daughter of Belle and F. G. Bonfils, cofounder of the *Denver Post*, fought her sister Helen over what May perceived as her fair share of their parents' multimillion-dollar estates. Lawsuits, trials, and out-of-court settlements awarded May her 50 percent. Then she built a lavish Jefferson County mansion, Belmar, where she lived in solitary splendor after twice divorcing her husband. Later she married her interior designer, who, after May's death, created from their assets the philanthropic Bonfils-Stanton Foundation, which continues to dispense millions of dollars annually to the state's nonprofit organizations. May's personally driven legacy serves only Colorado and Coloradans.

Born and raised in the awesome shadow of her notorious father, the obedient Helen Bonfils led a semi-austere life until his death in 1933. Then her many talents blossomed. She became an active force in the *Denver Post*; her love for the arts and especially for theater led her to a busy life in Denver theaters and on Broadway. With her inheritance and friendship with Broadway producers, she produced a number of smash hits, directed her talents and money to bringing New York City theater to Central City and the Elitch Gardens summer stock theater, and built the Bonfils Theater near City Park. "Bountiful Helen" contributed millions of dollars of her fortune to Colorado charities, religious and educational beneficences, civic enterprises, and countless humanitarian undertakings that never were made known to the public. After her death, the Helen G. Bonfils Foundation, with its enormous resources, then devoted all its giving to her final legacy, the Denver Center for the Performing Arts.

In western history, Caroline Bancroft was both literally and figuratively a giant. Just as she loomed over most women and many men in stature, so did she tower over other regional history writers of her time. Her twenty-two booklets supplied Coloradans and tourists with readable, relatively accurate information that educated readers about what it means to be a westerner. When Caroline proclaimed herself the "grande dame of Colorado history," few of the many who disagreed were brave enough to argue otherwise. She was an opinionated, colorful character who led a spartan life, supported largely by her own writing. The way Caroline lived revealed a woman who cared more about Coloradans and preserving their history than about her own personal comfort. She willed her estate and priceless collection of vintage photographs, family memorabilia, and books to the

Western History Department of the Denver Public Library and the Colorado Historical Society.

One of Caroline's best friends was the beautiful, irreverent Mary Coyle Chase, who invented an invisible rabbit more than six feet tall. He, in turn, made her rich and famous. Mary wrote *Harvey* to cheer up a neighborhood widow who had lost her son serving in the South Pacific in World War II. Her warm and sensitive play about a giant white rabbit enjoyed one of the longest runs (1,775 performances) on Broadway and not only made her neighbor laugh, it also won Colorado's first Pulitzer Prize in 1945. Mary's first career began at the *Rocky Mountain News* in the 1920s when she was a teenager. She became one of the best reporters ever to work in Denver, covering fires, shootings, murder trials, high society parties, and local prizefights. She was important in Denver because of the role she played at a thriving newspaper, her wit, her literary skill, and making a grieving mother laugh.

History is story first, the tales of past generations of people who made and shaped events. Knowing the stories of prominent early Coloradans strengthens our own sense of place and heightens our appreciation of where we live and why we live here. The more we learn about our home, perhaps the better we will take care of it. Philosopher/poet George Santayana knew this. His belief in the bedrock need for an informed citizenry is carved on the entrance to the University of Colorado's Norlin Library in Boulder: "He who knows only his own generation remains always a child." Coloradans—and there are millions more today—must know the past to understand the present, must be informed about critical issues like education, aridity, and preservation, for example, in order to give future Coloradans the same quality of life we were so lucky to inherit.

The six colorful, high-achieving women are worth knowing. They have impacted the lives of three or more generations of Coloradans. Yet, none of these women has a published biography. I was able to gain access to primary sources for each woman: through interviews with them or their family members and friends, and through research in manuscripts, printed source collections, and oral history recordings in Colorado. Their lives reveal an evolving city and state whose women helped shape—and raise—their home and ours.

She Decided "Who's Who in Denver Society"

Louise Sneed Hill
(1861–1955)

The acknowledged queen of Denver society stands by the staircase of her palatial home, built in 1905–1906 on the southwest corner of East Tenth Avenue and Sherman Street. (Photo: Harry M. Rhoads) (Western History Department, Denver Public Library)

S he was a short woman who wore spiked high-heeled shoes and high-crowned hats in her mansion's drawing room at 969 Sherman Street in Denver. She didn't like her stubby hands, so she wore elbow-length gloves to hide them. This vivacious southern belle didn't like Denver much, either, when she came to the city as a bride in 1895. "A social wasteland" she called it.

What the fabulously rich Mrs. Crawford Hill especially despised was a boring life. What she did to escape it shocked the Old Guard, Denver's reigning first families, and gave the town enough gossip to fill its post-Victorian ear. In the process Louise Sneed Hill became the social arbiter of Denver high society, leading her Sacred 36 friends on a merry-go-round of parties that lasted fifty years.

This glamorous woman entertained royalty and the international set, dazzling Denverites unused to such opulence. Social climbers drooled over her society page monopoly, courted her favor, and cherished invitations to her parties. World War I, the Great Depression, and Prohibition didn't faze Louise. But then neither did her husband's lingering illness nor her polo-playing lover's suicide.

Ironically, this woman who was dedicated to luxurious living inadvertently gave Denver an institution that endures while others who served a larger public have disappeared. For example, couples can no longer dance to big bands in the Elitch Trocadero Ballroom and children can't ride the Mister Twister roller coaster, because Elitch Gardens is dead. The city's public transportation system of electric trolleys running on steel tracks has been replaced by diesel buses. Elegant downtown institutions such as Daniels & Fisher and Neusteter's department stores are gone. But the social directory this self-proclaimed doyenne of society dictated to her personal secretary in 1908 remains. "Denver's first Social Record, 'Who's Who In Denver Society'" had 111 pages with more than 2,000 names. Now called the *Blue Book*, it continues to be published annually. Many regard it as a social accolade.[1]

Louise Bethell Sneed was born into southern aristocracy in 1861. After her parents died, the young woman with light brown hair and gray eyes moved to Memphis, Tennessee, to live with her older sister.

The Reconstruction South offered Louise little in the way of eligible wealthy gentlemen, and when her cousins, the W. D. Bethells, invited the maturing belle to Denver in 1893, Louise, age thirty two, jumped at the chance to expand her matrimonial horizons.

Although the Silver Crash severely limited the national economy and Denver was particularly depressed, the Old Guard turned out in black tie for a ball feting the Memphis visitor. The Bethell castle at East Colfax Avenue and Marion Street was an ornately gabled and turreted three-story structure that crowned Capitol Hill. Denver's social elite rode in horse and buggy to meet the southern beauty. Those men and their families who have become place-names in Colorado history included the John Iliffs, the Walter Cheesmans, the David Moffats, the John Evanses, and US Senator and Mrs. Nathaniel P. Hill.

Senator Hill's stained-glass portrait hangs in the State Capitol, because he was Colorado's first Republican US senator (1879–1885). Hill's immense fortune began in Black Hawk, where he built the first ore-processing smelter in the Rocky Mountains and then others at Alma and Argo. Hill and his partners often realized annual profits of a half million dollars or more from gold and silver extraction. The former professor of chemistry at Brown University in Providence, Rhode Island, lived in sedate luxury in Denver as he diversified his greatly expanding fortune.

Crawford Hill, the heir apparent, was Denver's most eligible bachelor, and Louise knew it. What he lacked in personality, the engaging Louise more than compensated for, especially her profound appreciation of wealth and power. In 1895, Louise and Crawford were married in an extravagant Memphis ceremony, and the Hill family newspaper, the *Denver Republican*, dutifully praised the bride's beauty in her pearl-white satin and chiffon gown. "Sparkling

Crawford Hill. (Western History Department, Denver Public Library)

9

on her ensemble," the society page revealed, "were superb diamonds, a gift from the groom."

Marrying Crawford Hill was one of Louise's most strategic social coups, but her new mother-in-law recognized the power play. Later, Alice Hale Hill confided to friends that she was "sick over Crawford's marriage."[2]

The newlyweds moved into La Veta Place, a fashionable row of large Victorian brownstone apartments at 1407 Cleveland Place, now Denver's Civic Center. La Veta Place, acquired by Augusta Tabor through her divorce settlement with H.A.W. Tabor, seemed dark and uninspired to the new bride. Louise was bored by at-home teas where the wives of Denver's social leaders entertained, and she ignored their charities and church work. While Old Guard member Anne Evans labored to build an art museum and Jean Chappel Cranmer sustained a symphony orchestra, Louise went to their benefit balls simply to dress up and be seen.

Crawford didn't seem to mind that his wife's determination to lighten the social scene and become Denver's social leader strained family harmony. When Nathaniel was born in 1896 and Crawford, Jr., was born in 1898, Louise became the power on the throne. She began serving champagne at luncheons, ignored Old Guard convention by courting the press and actively seeking publicity, and sent gifts to reporters who wrote stories about her parties. She took herself very seriously.

Louise dismayed the Hill family, particularly Crawford's two sisters, who resented the social competition. City newspapers hyped the tempest—"Denver Rent By Fiercest War Ever In West!" and "Millions To Be Spent!"—in the struggle over society's top position. Senator Hill's daughters were no match for Louise. The *Denver Republican* was sold, in part to stop the family feud, and her two sisters-in-law eventually left town.

While the ladies of the Old Guard were listening to Monday Forum lectures and attending exclusive Colonial Dames affairs, Louise and friends DiPazza Willcox (Mrs. Charles McCallister) and Agnes Tammen (Mrs. Harry H.) were lunching at the new Denver Country Club, riding to Colorado Springs where Julie Penrose (Mrs. Spencer) entertained them in her Broadmoor mansion, or dressing for the Sunday matches on the Polo Grounds. Society columnists filled their pages with pictures of the fashionable spectators. Louise could always be counted on to provide copy: "Mrs. Crawford Hill, as usual, looked stunning in her black and white striped chiffon gown, which is the Frenchiest thing in Denver," reported a *Rocky Mountain News* society editor.

And the coterie played bridge—the card game that explains the Sacred 36 title. There never were merely thirty-six people in the Hill circle, but one morning a reporter, desperate for a story, telephoned Louisa Morris (Mrs. P. Randolph) at her 707 Washington Street home, later Helen Bonfils's residence. "There were just the regular nine tables of bridge at Mrs. Hill's," Morris said.

"But who were they? What were their names?" the reporter persisted.

"Goodness, you'd think we were sacred, the way you're asking," Mrs. Morris replied.

The next day's society page headline read, "Party at Mrs. Hill's for the Sacred 36!" The label stuck.[3]

In 1905, Crawford Hill bought a half block on the southwest corner of East Tenth Avenue and Sherman Street for $20,000. He com-

The eighteenth-century-style Hill mansion (now law offices) features a sixteen-foot tall mirror, ornately framed in gold leaf, that must be removed by a derrick when the walls are painted. (Western History Department, Denver Public Library)

Liveried servants provided transportation for Louise Hill before the advent of the automobile. (Western History Department, Denver Public Library)

missioned Theodore Boal, who had designed the Denver Country Club and the Grant-Humphreys mansion at East Eighth Avenue and Pennsylvania Street, to design an eighteenth-century stone mansion for the site. While other mansions sprouting on Capitol Hill were imitative in design and marked more by exuberance than aesthetics, the Hill mansion (now law offices) was remarkable for its classic restraint.

The stately structure facing north opens onto a reception hall with black and ivory marble floors; to the right, winding marble stairs flare to hold an orchestra. To the left, a seventy-two-foot drawing room and a dining room open to a solarium that doubles as a ballroom. Each of the mansion's twenty-two rooms reflected Louise's love of luxury. The drawing room still holds a sixteen-foot-tall mirror, ornately framed in gold leaf, that must be removed by a derrick when the walls are painted.

Louise imported the furnishings for her new home, as well as a New York City dancing teacher who instructed her guests in the latest steps. Doing the "Grizzly Bear" and the "Turkey Trot" fascinated the Sacred 36. While the Old Guard was scandalized by such revelry, Louise entertained nonstop. The *Republican* noted: "There were men in the '36' who belong to the busy rich and they are racking their

Mrs. Crawford Hill, ca. 1908, in a gown designed for her presentation to King Edward VII at the Court of St. James, Buckingham Palace, London. Diamonds embellished her gold tiara, gown, and red velvet robe as she became the first Denverite to bow before a king. (Western History Department, Denver Public Library)

Mrs. Crawford Hill poses with her sons Crawford Jr. (left) and Nathaniel, ca. 1905. As adults the sons chose to live in Newport, RI. (Western History Department, Denver Public Library)

brains as to how they are going to get down to the office and not miss the dance in the morning. They are demanding invitations be for 7 A.M. This would give them at least an hour for dancing."

Louise filled her house with flowers. Before a party, greenhouse trucks delivered lilies, roses, and palm trees that turned the rooms into bowers. At just the right moment, the hostess would descend the dramatic staircase dressed in her favorite colors of black and white as an orchestra announced her presence. Denverites were awed by a whole new paradigm of at-home entertaining.

In 1907, Denver retained much of its frontier character. Many residents could clearly remember seeing Indian tipis on the banks of the South Platte River. Newspapers lured readers with stories of daring heroes: race car driver Barney Oldfield driving faster than a mile a minute at Overland Park, Ivy Baldwin performing trapeze acts beneath hot-air balloons at Elitch Gardens, and Buffalo Bill (Colonel William F. Cody) taking his Wild West show abroad and giving command performances for European royalty.

Now Louise Hill threw her hat into the ring and became another international celebrity. She used her friendship with the American ambassador to England to secure an invitation to be presented to King Edward VII at the Court of St. James in London. Explaining that her reception at Buckingham Palace "would give distinction for Denver Society," she became the first Denverite to bow before a king. Londoners marveled at the fine manners of this "Woman from the West"—clearly no social kin to Buffalo Bill. Wearing a white satin gown embroidered with diamonds, a diamond tiara, and a red velvet train trimmed in fourteen-karat gold, Louise impressed London and Denver gentry. (After her death, the velvet train was sold at a public auction for $22.50 to Jessica McDowell, a Denver interior designer. Colorado historian Caroline Bancroft retrieved the robe by paying McDowell $100, and after being reimbursed by the Hill sons, Bancroft donated the garment to the Colorado Historical Society.)[4]

In 1911, Louise became the first in Denver to entertain a US president when William Howard Taft came to town. She invited the Sacred 36, the Old Guard, and others to 969 Sherman. Red carpet extended to the curb for President Taft. Throngs of the uninvited watched the two Hill sons, dressed in white satin suits, greet him at the front door. Inside, an orchestra played as scores of seated guests peered through lavish table bouquets to glimpse the guest of honor and his hosts.

Money, not morals, dictated whom the arbiter of Denver society included in her social register. "First you must have the money. Then you must have the knowledge to give people a good time," Louise said. Between trips to Europe, polo matches, and parties, in 1908 the doyenne of society dictated a social register, *Who's Who in Denver Society*, that spelled out who was socially acceptable in Denver. She listed herself, her family, and her Sacred 36 friends first.[5] The first edition featured a full-page frontispiece of Louise in her court presentation gown. The 1908 book was bound in red cloth with gold lettering but was later changed to a blue cover and is known as the *Blue Book*.

The doyenne of Denver society listed more than 2,000 cross-indexed names of socially prominent residents in various categories, including: "Pioneers in the Social Field," "The Smart Set," "The Married Set," "Worth over a Million," and "Types of Denver Beauty," where Louise included herself and family first. Other pages were devoted to "Correct Conventions and Etiquette Up-to-Date," with rules for the calling card, proper hours for calling, the wedding journey, the high tea, and advice about getting into "Society" and staying there.

Glamorous Denverites liked being included. Henry Blackmer was one, and during Prohibition sent Louise cases of champagne from Paris; he had moved to France following his indictment in the Teapot Dome oil scandal. Others were Edna and Claude Boettcher, who turned 400 East Eighth Avenue into a small palace and later gave it to the state of Colorado for a governor's mansion. And Bulkeley Wells, the dashing, polo-playing mining engineer who epitomized Louise's definition of glamour, became her lover.

With his tight jodphurs and Rudolph Valentino good looks, Wells was a storybook prince made to order for a woman in search of a good time. A brigadier general in the Colorado National Guard, Wells was president of the great Smuggler-Union mine which produced $50 million dollars in gold from 1902 to 1923. Backed by financiers Harry Payne Whitney of New York City and Well's father-in-law, Colonel Thomas Livermore of Boston, Wells was riding high, wide, and handsome when Louise met him.

Wells and his proper wife, Grace, lived in Colorado Springs and belonged to such exclusive organizations as the Cheyenne Mountain and El Paso Clubs as well as the Denver Club and the Denver Country Club. Mutual interests drew the couples together, but Louise's fascination with Bulkeley cemented the relationship.

By 1914, Wells had an office apartment in Denver. Partygoers at the Country Club remember Bulkeley and Louise leaving the dance floor and disappearing upstairs. Crawford Hill didn't appear to object. In fact, for years husband, wife, and lover were a congenial trio, dining and traveling together.[6] Louise even hung a life-sized portrait of Bulkeley in his polo costume next to her husband Crawford's portrait in the mansion's reception hall.[7]

In 1918, Grace Livermore Wells divorced her husband on grounds of desertion, and Wells's luck began to run out. With Whitney and Colonel Livermore backing Wells in mining speculations from Canada to Mexico, the gambling engineer could afford to lose the estimated $15 million he had invested in the Old Comstock mine of Virginia City, Nevada, the Radium Company mine in Montrose County, Colorado, and lesser mining ventures. However, with the breakup of his marriage, Wells lost the Livermore financing that had helped bring him such phenomenal success. He resigned as president of the Smuggler-Union. But he continued to carry thousand-dollar bills in his pockets, which jingled with gold coins. Then disaster struck.

Crawford Hill, who had been ill for several years, died of heart failure in 1922. Instead of marrying Louise, now sixty-one, Wells surprised society by eloping with a young, beautiful, platinum-blond divorcee from Nevada. When Louise heard of the marriage she vowed, "I'll break him." And she did.[8]

Louise cut all ties with her former lover and persuaded her close friend, Harry Payne Whitney, to withdraw his financial backing of Wells. Without the Livermore and Whitney resources, Wells could no longer sustain his mining empire. He continued to gamble at cards and oil and gas speculations but lost heavily. With all his investments tumbling down around him, Wells saw only poverty as a prospect, and he couldn't face it. He went to his San Francisco office in May 1931 and wrote a note: "As a result of all my difficulties and worries, my mind is bound to go. Nothing but bankruptcy is possible as far as my estate is concerned. Do what you can for Mrs. Wells." Then he lay down on a couch and shot himself in the head.[9]

Later, when Louise was entertaining the press at cocktails, the irrepressible *Rocky Mountain News* photographer Harry Rhoads asked, "By the way, Mrs. Hill, whatever happened to Bulkeley Wells?"

"Well, I really don't know," the merry widow replied cheerfully.[10]

Although the Depression inconvenienced the Sacred 36, it didn't greatly afflict them. Louise occasionally shared her maids and butler with the troubled wealthy, and she fretted over the New Deal. She continued to travel, especially to Newport, Rhode Island, where her married sons lived. In a 1936 letter to her niece she wrote: "I expect to return to New York early in September, and may go abroad in October, as the children say—'My mother goes abroad for the weekend,' as I go only to Paris and, perhaps, to London. Denver is just the same. We dine out every night, and most of the people play bridge every day."[11]

Louise Hill never told anyone her age, and when it crept up on her, she defied the years as energetically as she welcomed a good, big party. Her "second maid," Nina Price, applied "tie-ups," a face-lifting device before the days of plastic surgery.[12] Dismissing age as dull and definitely not amusing, Louise said: "I was born in North Carolina where a girl becomes sixteen when she's about twelve or fourteen. She stays sixteen until she's twenty-one and she remains twenty-one until she's thirty. Finally she's eighty-five and she tells everyone she's a hundred."[13]

Running the Sherman Street mansion became overwhelming, and in the early 1940s Louise moved with her staff into the Brown Palace Hotel, owned by her great friend Claude Boettcher. Storing her silver fox and sable furs at Daniels & Fisher signaled an end to an extraordinary social life that Louise had turned into a vocation. Denver's most glamorous era ended when she died in 1955.

What was once the city's most distinct and visible social set is now a fragment of its former self. The conservative real estate, investment, and banking families who originally dominated the city's social scene are now mostly anonymous first-family descendants who shun publicity. They entertain in private clubs or at home behind locked gates. As former mayor William McNichols put it, "They saw it coming and relinquished their power."[14] Louise's perception of society is obsolete. Local historian Caroline Bancroft underscored that fact, and pronounced, "There is no society in Denver anymore."

What hasn't changed is the annual publication of the *Blue Book*, although you can't buy it at local bookstores because the social register is not for public sale. Listings in the book's roster remain highly exclusive, perceived by many as a measure of achievement. Louise couldn't have known in 1908 that she was creating an institution that would continue into the twenty-first century. She might not have cared.

Nevertheless, her wit, charm, and high society leadership commanded attention for fifty years. Louise's stubborn intent to lift a dusty, complacent cowtown to a high level of elegance obviously struck an admiring chord in Coloradans. During her reign there was glamor and fun, champagne and caviar, gossip and French couture. The champagne was more bubbly then, and the orchestra didn't stop playing at midnight.

Louise once instructed her audience that in order to be amusing, "First, you've got to have money." Still, as Lord Melbourne said after receiving the Royal Order of the Garter, England's highest accolade, "There was no damned nonsense of merit about it."

Roaring Twenties novelist F. Scott Fitzgerald fashioned his moth-like characters in *The Great Gatsby* and *Tender Is the Night* on the same insubstantial stuff as Louise Hill's silk chiffon, silver fox, and champagne. He believed that "the rich are different."

Louise Sneed Hill really was.

Notes

1. *Social Record of Denver*, 1948, Denver.
2. Nathaniel Hill Files, Western History Department, Denver Public Library.
3. Interview of Caroline Bancroft by Marilyn Griggs Riley, 1980.
4. Ibid.
5. Randy Welch, "Old Money Meets New Money," *Colorado Homes & Lifestyles*, January–February, 1984.
6. Interview of Caroline Bancroft by Marilyn Griggs Riley, 1980.
7. Crawford Hill Collection, Western History Department, Denver Public Library.
8. Interview of Caroline Bancroft by Marilyn Griggs Riley, 1980.
9. Jack Carberry, "Millions Gone, Bulkeley Wells, Picturesque Coloradan, Ends His Life," *Rocky Mountain News*, May 27, 1931.
10. Caroline Bancroft Interview by Marilyn Griggs Riley, June 1980.
11. Crawford Hill Collection, Western History Department, Denver Public Library.
12. Interview of Nina Price by Marilyn Griggs Riley, 1990.
13. *Denver Post*, May 30, 1955.
14. Randy Welch, "Old Money Meets New Money," *Colorado Homes & Lifestyles*, January–February, 1984.

Denver's Pioneering Physician and "Baby Doctor"

Justina L. Ford, MD
(1871–1952)

Dr. Justina Ford and her grandnephew Gene Carter, whom she had delivered in 1928, are photographed on the front porch of her Arapahoe Street home/medical office. Carter later became an elementary principal in the Denver Public Schools. (Western History Department, Denver Public Library)

Justina Ford, MD, Denver's and Colorado's first black female physician, applied in 1902 for a license to practice medicine in Colorado. The licensing examiner said, "I'd feel dishonest taking a fee from you. You've got two strikes against you. First off, you're a lady, and second, you're colored."

The thirty-one-year-old physician, keenly aware of the "two strikes," discreetly responded, "I know it. I thought it all through before I came. This is just the place I want to practice."[1] She joined her husband, the Reverend John E. Ford, who had moved from Chicago to Denver in 1899 to become pastor of the city's pioneer African-American Zion Baptist Church at East Twenty-Fourth Avenue and Ogden Street.[2] Justina, already licensed in Alabama and Illinois, became Colorado's first black woman physician on October 2, 1902, under medical license 3800. At the time, Denver's blacks numbered less than .03 percent of the city's population, and she was one of only five black physicians in the state.[3]

Justina specialized in obstetrics, gynecology, and pediatrics for fifty years. Her early practice required taking health care to her patients, arriving at their homes by bicycle, horse and buggy, or trolley. In 1911 she bought a two-story red brick house at 2335 Arapahoe Street and converted part of the first floor into office, waiting, and examining rooms that witnessed a steady flow of walk-in patients. Justina lived and practiced on Arapahoe Street for the rest of her life. Over a half century, she estimated, she delivered "more than 7,000 babies," or approximately three per week. Each baby became a member of the prestigious "Justina Baby Club," a listing prized by black, white, Mexican, Greek, Italian, German, Korean, Japanese, and Bohemian members. The common denominator among her patients was income, not race. Nearly all were poor.

Besides being female in a male-dominated profession, Justina had the formidable career obstacle of building a practice in a Denver medical community that was hostile to black physicians and dentists. Like the American Dental Association, "the American Medical Association barred membership to physicians who were not members of their local and state chapters, effectively excluding African-American physicians in 17 southern states" and elsewhere, including the state of Colorado.[4] Justina was not a member of the AMA because she did not belong to the Colorado Medical Society, and she could not join the

Colorado Medical Society or the Denver Medical Society because neither accepted blacks.[5]

Actually, race was the greatest strike against Justina and the only explanation for her exclusion from state and local medical societies. Women physicians had been licensed in Denver long before she had applied. In fact, decades before Justina moved to Denver, Alida Avery was Colorado Territory's first woman physician, licensed to practice before 1876, the year Colorado joined the Union. Edith Root was the first woman to be awarded her Colorado medical license, number 89. Avery, Root, and Mary Barker Bates were licensed and admitted to the Denver Medical Society in 1881. Eleanor Lawney, Colorado's first medical school graduate, was licensed to practice in 1888. Avery, Root, Bates, and Lawney belonged to local and national medical organizations, but all four women were white.[6]

For forty-eight years Justina fought to join the local medical societies because without membership, she was barred from staff privileges in most hospitals, including Denver General Hospital/Denver Health. In 1950, two years before her death, both local societies granted her membership.[7] At that point she became a staff member of Denver General Hospital and other hospitals. Justina's persistence as well as changes in public attitudes toward race, ethnicity, and gender finally had prevailed. The "Baby Doctor" who had fought an epic battle finally won.

JUSTINA LAURENA FORD, M. D.

Dr. Ford was born in Knoxville, Illinois, January 22, 1871, and died at her home in Denver, Colorado, October 15, 1952.

She acquired her preliminary education in Galesburg, Illinois, and her medical training in Chicago, earning her degree in 1899. After spending some time as a hospital director in Normal, Alabama, she came to Denver in 1902 and engaged in general practice until the date of her death. She had been a member of Denver County, Colorado State Medical Societies and the American Medical Association since 1950.

- - - *(colored)*

Copied from the Denver Medical Bulletin, January, 1953, for the Colorado Medical Society by Bradford Murphey, M.D., Historian.

Information about Justina L. Ford from the Denver Medical Bulletin. *(Colorado State Medical Society Library)*

Unfortunately, not much is known about Justina's early life. Pieces of her professional life are scattered throughout the Denver Public Library Western History Department, the Blair-Caldwell African American Research Collection of the Denver Public Library, and the Colorado Historical Society. The youngest of seven children, Justina Laurena Warren Ford Carter was born to Melissa and Pryor Warren on January 22, 1871, in Knoxville, Illinois, and grew up in nearby Galesburg. Blacks desperate for medical care often came to the Warren home at night for help from Justina's mother, a nurse. According to Gene Carter, Justina's nephew, Melissa Warren never turned anyone away, and the young Justina frequently assisted her mother in the care of patients.[8]

Justina was a determined, headstrong child, characteristics that served her well in her goal to become a doctor. As a child she refused to play with her brothers and sisters unless the game was "Hospital." "I wouldn't even play that unless they let me be the doctor. I didn't know the names of any medicines," and so she invented them, Justina told reporter Mark Harris. She also recalled that "when neighbor folks were ill I liked to tend them. I hope I didn't do them any harm," she chuckled, her face creasing in laughter that accentuated prominent cheekbones.

Justina's determination to become a doctor in the nineteenth century was a lofty goal for a black female. Pre-Emancipation black women had worked as apprentices and assistants to white physicians, and midwives had delivered babies long before the practice of obstetrics was established. Nonetheless, black women were generally barred from formal medical training. Dr. Rebecca Lee in 1864 and Dr. Rebecca J. Cole in 1867 were the first American black women to graduate from medical schools, but women of any color in American medicine were rare until the 1950s.[9]

The desire for equal rights in medicine was a corollary of social reform in the United States during the 1840s and 1850s. Early feminists saw admittance of women to medicine a dramatic case for their whole movement of temperance, antislavery, and equal rights. The Women's Medical College of Pennsylvania, which opened in 1850 in Philadelphia, was the only such school in the western world. "Doctresses," as its graduates were called, nonetheless encountered long delays in appointments to hospital staffs.

Prominent feminist Sara Josepha Hale championed the case for the whole women's movement in 1852. Editor of the popular *Godey's Ladies Book*, Hale attacked the medical community when she wrote in her influential magazine, "Talk about medicine being the appropriate sphere for man and his alone! With tenfold more plausibility and reason, we say it is the appropriate sphere for women and hers alone."[10] But progress was slow for aspiring women physicians and for blacks of either gender. Dr. Shryock reports that by 1910, just sixty-six American women were medical doctors. Justina was one of them.

Racial segregation impacted nearly every aspect of American culture, and medical school enrollment mirrored the status quo. In 1910, there were 3,409 African-American male physicians in the entire nation. Most of them had graduated from the seven all-black medical schools in existence.[11] Fortunately for Justina, she had completed her medical school education from Chicago's black Hering Medical School and had passed the state licensing examination before the school closed its doors after publication of the "Flexner Report."

Justina Ford's application for her Colorado medical liscense. (Colorado State Medical Society Library)

The prestigious Carnegie Foundation directed educator Abraham Flexner to research the quality of medical school education, and in 1910 his major study was published as "The Medical Education of the Negro" in *Medical Education in the United States and Canada: A Report to the Carnegie Foundation of the Advancement of Teaching.* It documented inadequate staffing and equipment and the high failure rate of graduates of black medical schools to pass state licensing examinations. The Flexner Report strongly influenced the closing of the mostly church-supported black medical schools in America and Hering Medical School. Just two southern schools, Meharry Medical College in Nashville, Tennessee, and Howard University College of Medicine in Washington, D.C., survived to educate black professionals. White medical schools accepted few black applicants and black physicians found themselves increasingly isolated from the mainstream of their profession.[12]

In 1892, as Justina was beginning her education at Hering, she married the Reverend John Ford, pastor of a Chicago Baptist church. After graduation, she was assigned to a hospital for a two-year internship in Normal, Alabama, where resistance to racial and gender integration was fierce. Her advisor pleaded with the reluctant Justina to take the assignment and "treat the colored" who were dying from whooping cough, tuberculosis, and other diseases because of lack of medical care. After completing the internship and despite its need for an able physician, "The Alabama community rejected Ford as a doctor on the grounds of race and gender," reports Jessie Carrie Smith in *Notable Black American Women.*

Justina joined her husband in Denver in 1902; she wanted to live where blacks could be a more integral part of the community. She believed that "Denver had a better attitude about color lines" and attributed this perception in part to the presence of the University of Denver and Regis College, which had helped break down racial attitudes. Denver looked like the right place because it was still "something of a pioneer town. I tell folks I came to Denver in time to help them build Pike's Peak, and it's almost the truth," she told journalist Mark Harris. Justina's mentor was Dr. William J. Cottrell, a black physician whose offices were at 1090 Nineteenth Street.[13] In 1903, Justina delivered her first Denver baby, Josephine Porter. After Cottrell's death in 1905, she assumed his practice.

At the turn of the twentieth century, Justina was correct in describing Denver "as something of a pioneer town" in terms of urban disorder, "a pattern established during the westward migrations, when sickness was the #1 killer, more prevalent than starvation, exposure, and accidents combined. Epidemics of diptheria, smallpox, typhoid and cholera plagued residents in Denver."[14]

Justina's commitment to healing the sick in Denver was as fervent as her husband's devotion to his ministry. The Fords separated in 1907, when the Reverend, with degrees from Fisk University, Beloit College, and the University of Chicago, was asked to serve a Baptist church in Jacksonville, Florida.[15] The Ford marriage, pulled by separate and demanding careers, ended in divorce. Justina kept her married name, by which she was professionally known.

By 1911, Justina had purchased an eight-room house at 2335 Arapahoe Street in the minority neighborhood of Five Points, where she lived and worked for the rest of her life. Five Points, immediately northeast of downtown Denver, is bounded by the South Platte River and Thirty-Eighth Avenue, Walnut and Downing Streets, Park

Dr. Ford's home after its relocation to 3091 California Street. The structure is now the home of the Black American West Museum, inspired by historian Paul Stewart. (Joyce B. Lohse)

Avenue West, East Twentieth Avenue, and Broadway. The roughly triangular area originally had been home to many prosperous white businessmen and professionals who had built elegant Victorian houses and mansions; smaller residences, however, were the norm. The city's increasingly polluted air, blanketing the neighborhood during winter thermal inversions in the river basin, as well as noise and congestion, led the first residents to move to higher ground, such as the Capitol Hill area. Minority families, mostly black and aware that there were places where they should not or could not go, replaced them. Five Points became a segregated neighborhood, "a world apart from ruling white Denver."[16]

Five Points was a "most stylish community" in Denver at the end of World War I. The landmark Rossonian Hotel, a music venue that drew audiences of all races for several generations, stood in the heart of Five Points at the triangular corner of Twenty-Seventh, Welton, and Washington. The Rossonian featured nationally acclaimed blues and jazz musicians like Billie Holiday, Louis Armstrong, Duke Ellington, Ella Fitzgerald, and James Brown. Private social clubs, like the Capri, established themselves nearby, drawn by the Rossonian magnet. The area became known as "Jazz City."

Five Points prospered. Laborers, railroad porters, and domestic workers joined black physicians and dentists, chiropodists and morticians in the bustling community. Three black newspapers, the *Colorado Statesman*, the *Denver Star*, and the *Denver Inquirer*, served the community. Barbershops, grocery stores, cleaning establishments, restaurants, and the Deep Rock Artesian Water and Bottling Co., founded in 1898, served the area and the larger city beyond. In this community of churches, Justina belonged to the Zion Baptist Church, founded in 1865 by ex-slaves. Zion's prominent pastor, Wendell T. Liggins, remembered that his friend Justina was "never late to services" and was one of Five Points' most beloved residents.[17]

"Dr. Ford took care of the neighborhood," remembers Roseanne Taht, who grew up across Arapahoe Street from Justina. Now a librarian at the Denver Public Library, Taht proudly displays a childhood souvenir, a scar on her scalp. "I fell off my bicycle and cut my head. It bled a lot, and Mother took me across the street. Dr. Ford sewed it up."[18]

Ruth Bradford, Taht's mother, remembers Justina with respect and affection. "Dr. Ford was always very professional and always kind. I knew her as an older woman; she was maybe five feet, four inches tall then. She was not skinny, just nice, and whenever she left her house, she always wore a dress and a hat." Bradford underscores Justina's professional bearing, recalling, "There was an accident on Twenty-Fourth and Arapahoe late one night. The sirens woke me, and I looked out the window to see what was happening. The lights were on in Dr. Ford's house, and I saw her walking down the street toward the accident. In the middle of the night, she was wearing a dress and a hat!"[19]

Justina's compassion was well-known. "Lots of babies were left on her doorstep. Dr. Ford took them to hospitals for care and adoption," Bradford recalls. Through Dr. Ford, another neighbor, Mrs. Frasier, a childless young widow who was unable to work because of severely ulcerated legs, adopted two young children. "Dr. Ford arranged for Mrs. Frasier to get aid for needy children so the three had money to live on. She was able to survive with state money, and the kids were well taken care of. Dr. Ford did all that so her neighbor could stay in her home." Later, Bradford recalled, "Dr. Ford gave Mrs. Frasier new medical treatment that helped her go back to work."

Despite being a woman in the male-dominated field of medicine, Justina managed to build a large clientele, thanks to the considerable numbers of poor and minorities who found their way to her office. In addition to these two groups of patients, whom she called "plain white and plain colored," there were sizable foreign-born groups in which the men often believed that a woman physician, rather than a man, should be in attendance at childbirth. From these groups came much of her following. Still, to Justina, determining racial percentages in her practice was unimportant. "Folks make an appointment and I wait for them to come or go to see them and whatever color they turn up that's the color I take them," she asserted.[20]

She was an equal opportunity doctor, according to retired assistant Denver fire chief Frank Quintana. "Her patients were largely members of ethnic communities. She delivered me, my sister and an uncle." He remembered her dedication, recalling that she once spent the night helping a family through a stillbirth. When she was paid, she often used the money for groceries for the patient and family. "I don't know how she survived money-wise," said Quintana, who was born in 1932. "During that period there was no money around. There were a lot of Hispanic workers. They knew nothing about how or where to get a doctor. My uncle spoke Spanish, and he was head of a railroad work gang. He got paid pretty well. So it was because of him that Dr. Ford birthed me and my sister. He sent her over."[21]

Few families had cars in those days, but the frugal Justina, who neither drove nor had a driver's license, later bought a sedan that family members drove. Her nephew, Jack Bradley, who became the first black member of the Denver Symphony Orchestra, often drove her on her rounds. Five Points residents remembered that when they saw the long black car pull up, they knew there was another baby on the way. Her nephew, Gene Carter, whom Justina had delivered in 1928, drove his aunt to patients on emergency calls and holidays. Justina's second husband, Alfred Allen, a cook for the Burlington Railroad, drove her too and also managed the household because her office was open six days a week and Sundays by appointment.

Dr. Ford prepares to make house calls to her patients. Family members drove her to patients' homes because she did not have a driver's license. (Black American West Museum)

She had her own routine for home deliveries, and it gained a mystique in Five Points. Nea Stoner described the "Baby Doctor" as a "small, plump woman" with tiny hands that could turn a baby without forceps. Justina delivered five of Stoner's nieces. "When it came time to deliver the baby, she took off her street clothes and delivered the baby in her slip or a gown" to protect the child from germs from her street clothes. Stoner also recalled, "If it took eight hours to deliver a baby, Dr. Ford would stay, talk to her patient, and wait for the baby to be born. Alfred Allen would wait in the car outside, and she would send her husband off to eat from time to time, but she wouldn't go. We would feed her. She was just a good human being." Carrie Scott remembers Ford as "a proper woman who always had on a whole lot of clothes, and she'd sit in our rocking chair during my mother's labor and give my father orders. And that was funny, watching my father, because he was such a macho man, and for this tiny little lady to come in like that and quietly give him instructions ..."[22]

"Her whole life seemed to be doctoring" and she was busy all the time, said Amanda Cousins Collins. Patients often sat quite a while in her waiting room before she could see them. "When I stayed at her house, though, we would sometimes play the piano and sing religious songs like 'Jesus Loves Me, This I Know.'"[23] Collins and other relatives who had lived with Justina clearly were impressed by her stern self-discipline. She enforced a daily "quiet hour" for reading medical journals in order to keep abreast of the latest treatments and technologies and a "telephone hour" to answer patients' questions—rules broken only by medical emergencies.

The "Baby Doctor" treated the ill and their struggling families. Nephew Gene Carter recalled a frequent detour after their trips to patients' homes. One bitterly cold day, Justina prescribed medicine for a family who had no food or heat. When the rounds were finished, she asked Carter to drive to the Lincoln Market at Twenty-Sixth Avenue and Welton Street. "She knew the grocer and they had a special signal for whenever she would come into the store," said Carter. "If she held up one finger to the grocer, that meant she wanted one bag of groceries from her prepared list. If she held up two fingers, that meant two bags. She held up two fingers and told the grocer to have the bags delivered to the family she'd seen that had no food." Ford and Carter also stopped at the neighborhood coal

The Lincoln Market at East Twenty-Sixth Avenue at Lincoln Street featured prominently in Dr. Ford's strategy to patients and their families who had no food. She and the grocer had silent signals to provide bags of groceries from a prepared list to be delivered to families she had just seen. (Wallace Yvonne Tollette)

company to order a half ton of coal for the family. "I asked her why she did that and she said there were people in need."[24]

Justina Baby Club members and others remember her soothing bedside manner. Pauline Allen was one of Justina's patients and remembered that "Dr. Ford was lovely, quiet, listened carefully to her patients, and spoke with a soft voice. It was always a nice experience. She would explain an illness calmly. I never saw her frustrated. She was an old-fashioned doctor who had some home remedies like garlic pills for gall bladders. We still feel her presence in our community."[25]

"Dr. Ford was the only doctor I ever knew," said Zepha Grant, age eighty-six. Justina delivered Grant in 1912 and later Grant's first child. "Dr. Ford always gave you that extra care. You just expected her to solve any illness you had," the grateful patient recalled. Grant was one of many neighborhood children who walked to Justina's house for treatment of aches and pains. She suffered from asthma, and Justina "spent many hours poring over professional texts for the most progressive treatments. She did so much for the people here. You didn't have to hand some money over to her right away, either.

Dr. Ford didn't send bills, she didn't even care about the bills—she just cared about you."[26]

Prenatal care and home delivery costs ranged from $15 to $30 in those days, and because most of her patients were low-income, the issue of payment was often problematic. "Folks pay," Justina said, "but not always right away. Sometimes they pay me in goods rather than in cash—groceries, poultry, and so forth—and some of the things they give me are more lasting than cash. Why, just look!" she told Mark Harris as she swung open the door leading to her reception room. Spread on a table was a brightly colored oriental cloth, and nearby a handwoven Mexican blanket covered a chair. "That's just a sample. You can't buy things like that. But most folks manage to get the cash somehow. They'll have it in a Bible maybe or tucked away in a tin can somewhere. There was one lady who couldn't pay for her baby until the baby was 13 years old. I'd forgotten about the bill, but she hadn't." Justina remembered "delivering a Spanish mother when she was very young—neither she nor the family had any money to pay me. The girl moved to California and I never thought any more about the matter. But when she was pregnant again, you know what she did? She came clear back to me. She wouldn't let anyone handle her but me. That's the kind of thing that makes a doctor proud."[27]

Jack Bradley lived with his parents in Justina's home and remembered the homegrown vegetables, poultry, pork, maintenance of Justina's house and garden, and other gifts from patients who could not pay in cash for medical services. "Her charity and good works were well known. Whenever she'd receive a personal gift," recalled Bradley, "she'd leave it in its box in her bedroom. You never saw her use the things. Eventually, she'd give it all away."[28]

Often Justina's house calls would take her to migrant farmworker's camps on the edges of the city and to other homes beyond Five Points. "Though a stern-visaged woman, whose authority was sharply defined," wrote Petra Lopez-Torres, "she gave the best care to mother and baby without needless waste of time and needless extras. No patient was left unattended as her care persisted for many days after delivery for 'surprise visits' at any time of day or night. She was the best baby doctor in town." Lopez-Torres remembers Justina's calls in lower downtown Denver. "She delivered four of my sister's children, and I was there when they were born. It was a long time ago, but I can still remember how her nephew would drive her to my sister's house at 1033 9th Street. The house is still standing in the middle of the Auraria campus in the 9th Street Park."[29]

Most of Justina's medical contemporaries delivered babies in hospitals; those who did not generally practiced in rural areas. Justina explained her home-delivery practice: "Here was a little one about to come on the scene and someone had to bring it, so why not me?" The babies, she continued, "were probably conceived at home, and have nowhere else to be born but at home."[30]

Justina, like other early minority physicians, was named to a staff position at Denver General Hospital, but only as an alternate, annually appointed adjunct, not as a tenured faculty member. An "alternate adjunct," according to Margie Bell Cook of the Black Nurses Association, meant that "you can't have the same, equal privileges as a white counterpoint, and others are looking over your shoulder" in the hospital.[31] In 1928, 1930, and 1932, for example, Justina held adjunct appointments.[32] Dr. John Sbarbaro, former deputy director for medical affairs, Department of Health and Hospitals, observed that "staff privileges" were defined by documented "specific skills" that physicians were allowed to perform. The policy's intent was to protect hospitals from lawsuits that could occur if a physician worked outside of professional credentialing.[33]

Justina recalled how she "fought like a tiger" for underserved populations and against racial barriers. She persisted in her struggle for medical collegiality and membership in the Denver and Colorado medical societies so that she could secure permanent hospital staff status. For decades she kept applying and, in December 1949, added a handwritten letter to her application to the Denver Medical Society:

> ... I do a lot of OB work, have delivered around 7,000 babies in the State of Colo. I assume many of their burdens and make many personal sacrifices. ... I need recognition in the medical society for personal help and to help you preserve the present system. ...
>
> I am known by many of Denver's best MD's. ... I always have help in Major surgery, such men as Drs. T.L. Williams, L.V. Sams, W.H. Halley, B.B. Jaffa and Dr. Kauvar. ...

Many patients wonder why I do not go to hospitals. I see it establishes an inferiority complex in their minds. It has required patience and fortitude to endure as I have, from 1902 to 1949.[34]

In 1950, two years before her death, both societies granted Justina membership, and she was then admitted to standard practice in hospitals.

Near the end of her life, Justina was formally honored for her long and distinguished medical service in Denver and its environs. In 1951 the Cosmopolitan Club awarded her its Human Relations Award. Later the Justina Ford Medical Society, comprising black medical students, faculty, and residents, was chartered at the University of Colorado. The Warren Public Library in northeast Denver was renamed the Ford-Warren Library in 1975, honoring her as a pioneering physician and humanitarian. Both the Denver Medical Society and the Colorado Medical Society passed resolutions honoring Ford posthumously "as an outstanding figure in the development and furtherance of health." The Colorado Medical Society further identified Justina as a "Colorado Medical Pioneer." In 1992, Historic Denver honored 100 spectacular Coloradans—including Dr. Justina Ford, Dr. Florence Sabin, Governor Ralph Carr, John and Mary Elitch, and educator Emily Griffith—who were recognized for "significant contributions to the formation of the State and lasting impressions on its people."[35]

Justina's strenuous life ended on October 14, 1952, when she died in her home weeks after delivering her last baby. She was eighty-one. The Denver community filled the Zion Baptist Church sanctuary to celebrate her life. She was buried in Fairmount Cemetery, where a modest gravestone, now nearly hidden by rosebushes, marks her plot. She was survived by her husband, Alfred Allen, nieces, and nephews.

Allen sold the house, left Denver, and later died in New Jersey; the empty Arapahoe Street home became a target for vandalism. Sandra Parrish of East-West Investment Partnerships identified 2342 Broadway Limited Partnerships as the absentee owner. "We all want it torn down because police are there all hours of the day dealing with drug dealers, illegal aliens, fires, everything under the sun," said Parrish.[36]

Paul Stewart, a local historian and founder of the Black American West Museum and Heritage Center, was furious about plans to demolish the home to make room for a parking lot. He and other admirers of Dr. Ford hastily organized a last-ditch effort to save the house. Denver City Councilman Hiawatha Davis, Elizabeth Schlosser of Historic Denver, and US Congresswoman Pat Schroeder joined the cause. Mayor Federico Peña and Historic Denver helped with arrangements to guarantee purchase of the structure, built in 1889. The preservation project gained substantial support from the Denver Housing Authority and the Community Development Agency.[37]

Early on the morning of February 7, 1984, the house was towed for a mile through city streets to its new location, a vacant lot at 3091 California Street. Four years later, now painted gray, it was restored and designated a Denver Landmark and listed on the National Register of Historic Places. Renamed the Black American West Museum and Heritage Center, the landmark displays Justina's medical offices and Paul Stewart's extensive historical collection of black cowboy artifacts. The renovated structure is open to the public and is also used as a community meeting place. In 1988 a nonprofit organization, Art at the Stations, installed a larger-than-life bronze bust of Justina at the Thirtieth Avenue and Downing Street light rail station across the street from her relocated house.

Denver artist Jess E. Dubois, who used to shine shoes as a young man living in Five Points, was commissioned to sculpt and cast the sculpture that portrays a young Justina holding a baby in her arms. DuBois never knew Justina, but she delivered many of his friends. "When I was young, I couldn't figure out why the Lady Doctor would stay here with us when she could have gone to Los Angeles or Chicago to make more money. But now I hold to the belief that she was truly God-sent. There were so many people that couldn't afford doctors, and she was the only doctor in the area."[38]

"Ain't No Grave," the old black gospel song that celebrates the power of a forceful human spirit over death, evokes Justina Ford's contributions to a better world. And she believed in that better world. "When all the fears, hate, and even death is over," she told Magdalena Gallegos, "we will really be brothers as God intended us to be in this land. For this I have worked all my life."

Application for Membership

DUPLICATE FOR REFERENCE TO STATE SOCIETY

To the officers and members of the _Denver Co._ Medical Society, a component of the COLORADO STATE MEDICAL SOCIETY:

Gentlemen: I hereby make application for _Active Junior_ membership in your Society,
(Class of Membership)
and, if accepted as a member, I agree to support the Constitution and By-Laws of your Society and of the COLORADO STATE MEDICAL SOCIETY, and the Principles and Ethics of the American Medical Association.

The accompanying $_____, when accepted, will include dues in your society and the COLORADO STATE MEDICAL SOCIETY until Dec. 31, 19____.

(Please print or typewrite the following information)

Name in full (no initials) _Justina Laurena Ford MD_
Residence Address _2335 Arapahoe St_
(Mark with a cross (X) which address the Society shall use for mailing Journals and notices)
Office Address _2335 Arapahoe St._
Date of Birth _1-22-71_ Place _Knoxville, Ill_ Race _Colored_
Preliminary Education _Galesburg Ills_
Medical College _Hering Medical School Chicago Ill_ Date of M.D. Degree _June 30-1899_
(Give name of College in full)
Other Degrees and Names of Schools Conferring them _____
Date of Colo. Medical License _1902_ Licenses in other State _Illinois & Alabama_ Dates _1899-1900_
Specialty if any _____
Internships Served _____
Previous residences since graduation, with approximate dates _Alabama 1900 — Colo 1902_

I have not previously held membership in any County Medical Society except in the _____
Medical Society, State of _____, from 19____ to 19____. I transferred, resigned in good standing, was dropped for non-payment of dues, was suspended, was expelled from the above Society in 19____.
(Cross out wrong words)

SIGNED _Justina Laurena Ford MD_ (date) _11 — 8 —_, 19_49_

(DO NOT LET CARBON PAPER GO BELOW THIS LINE)

To The Colorado State Medical Society Date_____ 19____

Gentlemen:
Please compare the above information, supplied by the Applicant, with your records and those of the Colorado State Board of Medical Examiners and the Biographic Department of the American Medical Association. Attachment of date and signature by an authorized representative of the Colorado State Medical Society, without comment, will indicate that the above information is correct and complete so far as your records show.
If your files contain additional information that will assist our Board of Censors in determining the above Applicant's qualifications for membership, we will appreciate receipt of such information by letter, which may be on the back of this sheet.

_____M.D., Secretary, _____Medical Society.

CK
ama
12/7/49

December 12 '49
No corrections or additions to date
Helen M. Avery
for The Colorado State Medical Society

Note: The State Society By-Laws require that this duplicate form be mailed to the Executive Secretary of The Colorado State Medical Society BEFORE the Component Society acts upon the above Application. It will be returned to the local secretary as soon as possible. AFTER it has been returned to the local secretary and its information noted by the Component Society, the Component Society may act upon the Application in any manner it sees fit under its own By-Laws.

*A copy of Dr. Ford's Application for Membership to the Colorado State Medical Society.
(Colorado State Medical Society Library)*

JUSTINA L. FORD, M. D.
2335 Arapahoe Street
Phone MAin 3619
Denver 5, Colorado

11/8/49

To Whom It Concerns.

I do general practice – Work among all classes & races – many are in the low income group – I do a lot of OB work have delivered around 7000 babies in the State of Colo –

I assume many of their burdens and make many personal sacrifices – To many of these people socialised medicine might be particularly attractive – I need recognition in the medical Society for personal help and to help you preserve the present system

I am known by many of Denver's best M.D. Please inquire – I would appreciate it.

I always have help in Major surgery, such men as Dr. T. Williams L. V. Sams – W. H. Halley – B. B. Jaffa and Dr. Kouvar, medical – Many patients wonder why I do not go to Hospitals – I see it establishes an inferiority complex in their minds –

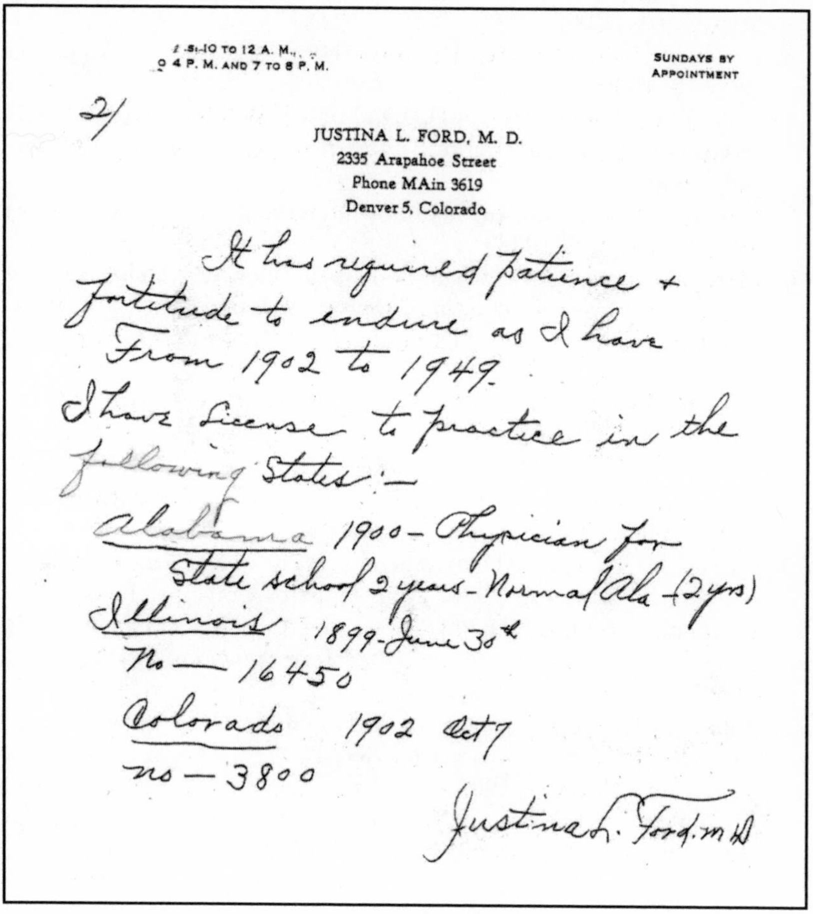

I -5.-IO TO I2 A. M.,
9 4 P. M. AND 7 TO 8 P. M.

SUNDAYS BY
APPOINTMENT

JUSTINA L. FORD, M. D.
2335 Arapahoe Street
Phone MAin 3619
Denver 5, Colorado

It has required patience + fortitude to endure as I have From 1902 to 1949.

I have License to practice in the following States:—

Alabama 1900 — Physician for State school 2 years - Normal Ala (2 yrs)

Illinois 1899 - June 30th
No — 16450

Colorado 1902 Oct 7
no — 3800

Justina L. Ford. m D

Dr. Ford's introduction letter to apply to the Denver Medical Society. (Colorado State Medical Society Library)

Notes

1. Mark Harris, "The 40 Years of Justina Ford," *Negro Digest*, March 1950.
2. Clementine Pigford, *Beautiful, Beautiful Zion!*, Custom Products and Sales, Aurora, 2003.
3. Colorado Medical Society, "Dr. Justina Ford," *Colorado Medicine*, February 15, 1989.
4. P. Preston Reynolds, MD, PhD, "Dr. Louis T. Wright and the NAACP: Pioneers in Racial Integration," *American Journal of Public Health*, June 2000.
5. Connie Johnson, "Dr. Justina Ford: Preserving the Legacy," *Odyssey West*, March/April 1988.
6. Marilyn Griggs Riley, "Champion of the Sick and Helpless," *The Women Who Made the Headlines*, Denver Woman's Press Club, 1998.
7. Colorado Medical Society, "Dr. Justina Ford," *Colorado Medicine*, February 15, 1989.
8. Connie Johnson, "Dr. Justina Ford: Preserving the Legacy," *Odyssey West*, 1988.
9. Lisa E. Thompson, MD, "Two Strikes: The Role of Black Women in Medicine Before 1920," Pharos Alpha Omega Alpha Honor Medical Society, Winter 1955, Henry Ford Hospital, Detroit.
10. Richard H. Shryock, MD, "Women in American Medicine," *Medicine in America: Historical Essays*, Johns Hopkins University Press, 1966.
11. P. Preston Reynolds, MD, PhD, "Dr. Louis T. Wright and the NAACP: Pioneers in Racial Integration," *American Journal of Public Health*, June 2000.
12. William S. Pierson, "Justina Ford, M.D.: Pushing Back the Frontiers," *Colorado Medicine*, February 15, 1989.
13. *Denver City Directory*, 1903.
14. Seymour E. Wheelock, MD, "Three Centuries in an Hour: An Overview of the History of Child Care in Colorado." In *For a Child's Sake: The History of The Children's Hospital, Denver, CO 1910–1990*, edited by Rickey Hendricks and Mark S. Foster, University Press of Colorado, 1994.
15. Pigford, *Beautiful, Beautiful, Zion!*
16. Phil Goodstein, *DIA and Other Scams: A People's History of the Modern Mile High City*, New Social Publications, 2000.
17. *5 Points Neighborhood, Historic Denver Guides*, Denver Neighborhoods History Project, 1995.
18. Interview of Roseanne Taht by Marilyn Griggs Riley, 2005.

19. Interview of Mrs. Ruth Bradford by Marilyn Griggs Riley, 2005.
20. Victoria Cooper, "Legendary Five Points obstetrician brought 7,000 youngsters into the world," *Rocky Mountain News*, February 22, 1991.
21. *Rocky Mountain News*, June 1, 1998.
22. *Ain't No Grave*, two-act drama based on the Dr. Justina Ford Oral History Project, funded by the Denver Public Schools and Paul Stewart, cofounder of the Black American West Museum, 1991.
23. Victoria Cooper, *Rocky Mountain News*, February 22, 1991.
24. Sheba R. Wheeler, "Beloved Doctor Gets Special Treatment," *Denver Post*, June 1, 1998.
25. *Zion Baptist Church*, video, Colorado Historical Society, 2000.
26. Sheba R. Wheeler, "Beloved Doctor Gets Special Treatment," *Denver Post*, June 1, 1998.
27. Harris, "The 40 Years of Justina Ford."
28. Jack Bradley Papers, Blair-Caldwell African American Research Collection, Denver Public Library.
29. Petra Lopez-Torres, "The Last of a Kind," *Urban Spectrum*, September 1988.
30. Colorado Medical Society, "Dr. Justina Ford."
31. Interview of Dr. Margie Bell Cook by Marilyn Griggs Riley, 2004.
32. *El Amigo*, annual publication of the Senior Class, Colorado Training School for Nurses, Denver General Hospital, 1932.
33. Interview of John Sbarbaro, MD, by Marilyn Griggs Riley, 2004.
34. Justina Ford letter, November 8, 1949, to the Denver Medical Society Association.
35. Colorado 100 Luncheon Program, Historic Denver, Inc., May 15, 1992.
36. Gary Gerhardt, "Historic house wins reprieve for three days," *Rocky Mountain News*, July 19, 1983.
37. Editorial, "Memorial to Justina Ford preserves Denver Heritage," *Rocky Mountain News*, September 24, 1988.
38. Sheba R. Wheeler, "Beloved Doctor Gets Special Treatment," *Denver Post*, June 1, 1998.

The Other Bonfils Daughter

Mary (May) Madeline Bonfils Stanton (1883–1962)

May Bonfils Stanton poses for her favorite portrait painted in 1947. Her necklace is possibly one that features the 70.2 carat diamond, "The Idol's Eye," set in platinum and surrounded by 35 total carats of smaller diamonds. (Western History Department, Denver Public Library)

Coloradans today know little about the life and contributions of May Bonfils Stanton, the elder daughter of the cofounder of the *Denver Post*. However, this feisty heiress affected the state's cultural, medical, and religious institutions through her extensive philanthropy. Her only sibling, Helen, was a dramatic, high-profile personality, while May Bonfils chose privacy and remains virtually unknown since her death in 1962.

Even longtime area residents are likely to: (1) mispronounce her name; (2) remember just her Jefferson County mansion, a western version of the Petit Trianon that Louis XVI built for his queen, Marie Antoinette; or (3) confuse May with her actress sister whose multimillion-dollar inheritance helped build the Denver Center for the Performing Arts in downtown Denver. That confusion would have enraged May. She scorned actors. To her, "Theater was for show-offs."

May, born in 1883, and Helen, born in 1889, were the only children of Belle Barton Bonfils and Frederick Gilmer (F.G.) Bonfils. Belle, a mild, dutiful wife, deferred to her husband, an explosive and dictatorial personality who became one of the nation's most notorious and reviled newspaper publishers. During their own stormy lifetimes, the daughters worked separately to soften their father's reputation through bountiful philanthropy. Charity between the two women, however, was impossible. Nourishing personal grievances, each ordered her lawyer to craft a mutual promise, signed by both women, that regardless of who died first, neither sister would protest entombment beside their parents at the Fairmount Cemetery Mausoleum. Neither May nor Helen bore children, and the F.G. branch of the Bonfils family tree ended when they died.

Not just a rich female, May Bonfils was a conspicuous anomaly in an era of demure womanhood and Gibson Girl sweetness. She was stubbornly independent, outspoken, and shrewd. If early Denver's social conventions restricted her freedom, she defied them. She ignored Denver's high society, which excluded her family. To escape from her possessive father's strict household rules, May eloped with the first man to propose marriage. Later she hired the best probate lawyer in town to break both parents' wills, which had rewarded Helen and punished May. Before her death in 1962, May sold her

Denver Post stock shares as a final insult to Helen—a decision that rocked the foundations of the "Voice of the Rocky Mountain Empire" and contributed to ending the newspaper's eighty-five years of local ownership.

How May Bonfils Stanton, despite her reclusive nature, impacted and disturbed twentieth-century Denver is a story of family dysfunction, extravagant lifestyle, and enduring philanthropy through a very personally driven legacy that benefits only Coloradans.

Every day thousands of vehicles heading east on Speer Boulevard at Emerson Street in Denver pass an antique marble fountain in Hungarian Freedom Park. The stately ornament with four stone lions couchant celebrates an eighteenth-century devotion to balance, proportion, and scale. Unattributed and neglected, the fountain is the only public artifact from May Bonfils's fabled Lakewood estate, Belmar. She created the name by combining a syllable of her mother's name and one from her own. May's dazzling white terra-cotta-faced manor west of Denver had twenty-two rooms.

In 1937 the prickly, fifty-four-year-old heiress, recently separated from her husband, purchased a square mile of rolling farmland with $200,000 from her inheritance and built Belmar. One of the West's great houses, the mansion stood at 777 South Wadsworth Boulevard in the tiny farming community of Lakewood. The rural site distanced her from Denver, her sister, and the *Denver Post*. For twenty years this privileged woman lived at Belmar in splendid seclusion, surrounded only by inanimate treasures: rare European antiques, Aubusson rugs, tapestries, marble statuary, and fine arts. When a friend asked why there were no contemporary pieces at Belmar, the owner imperiously dismissed the question. She clearly preferred an earlier time of romance and Old World royalty. "The Twentieth Century never existed," she declared.[1]

How F.G. amassed and allocated his self-made fortune is intrinsic to the lives of his daughters, genetic reflections of their willful, flamboyant father. His grandfather, born Buonfiglio, was a Corsican who had fought with Napoleon's armies and had emigrated to the United

States after Napoleon's defeat. Buonfiglio shortened the name to Bonfils. Young Bonfils attended the US Military Academy at West Point but left before graduating. He married Belle Barton of Peekskill, New York; the couple lived in F.G's hometown, Troy, Missouri, where May was born.

Bonfils's legitimate business ventures ended in failure. His marginal enterprises made money but were abruptly ended by the law. For example, in 1889 he envisioned making a profit in the homesteading rush into Oklahoma Indian territory. He paid $600 for a square mile of sagebrush across the border in the Texas panhandle. The land was seven miles from the nearest water and thirty-five miles from the nearest town. Bonfils platted the section into a town, named it Oklahoma City and advertised lots in Oklahoma City, Texas, at $2 to $25 each. In Bonfils's advertisements, "Oklahoma City" appeared in huge block letters, but "Tex." was in much smaller type. Unsuspecting people bought lots in Bonfils's town site, believing it to be Oklahoma City, Oklahoma, which was the location of a profitable Santa Fe Railroad station. He allegedly cleared $15,000 before the scheme was revealed as a fraud. He found it convenient to move his family to his wife's home in New York, where his second daughter, Helen, was born in 1889.[2]

By 1894, Bonfils was back in Kansas City, Kansas, operating lotteries. The main complaint about the legal lotteries was not that bribed officials looked the other way, but that no one seemed to win the big prizes, advertised to be as large as $15,000. Most of the big winners turned out to be friends or employees of Bonfils's lottery companies, which then advertised the winnings to stimulate the sale of more tickets. The *Kansas City Star* exposed the scheme, describing Bonfils as "formerly a Kansas City real estate swindler," but by then Bonfils had bank deposits totalling $130,000. In 1895 he pleaded guilty to violating Kansas vagrancy laws by loitering around a lottery and gambling house "without visible means of support." He paid the fines and went to Denver.[3]

F.G. moved to Colorado because he, like so many other fortune seekers, sensed limitless possibilities in the West. When the Bonfils family arrived in Denver, they liked the little boomtown that hadn't yet come of age. Their house at 939 Corona Street in the fashionable Capitol Hill neighborhood was a quiet place to raise their six- and twelve-year-old daughters. Denverites were recovering from the Silver Crash of 1893 and were content to live peacefully. "They sipped hot toddies around winter fireplaces and dozed in tree-shaded summer backyards. Only a good view of the mountains seemed important."[4]

Bonfils wanted a lot more than a mountain view. He wanted to make money. For Bonfils, according to Gene Fowler's *Timber Line, A Story of Bonfils and Tammen*, "Money was Power and Power was God Almighty." With his new partner, Heye Heinrich (Harry) Tammen, he made a fortune and a lifelong friend. The men shook hands on their purchase of the failing *Evening Post* and renamed it the *Denver Post*. Located at 1019 Sixteenth Street, the office site is now part of the block occupied by the Prudential Plaza. Although neither claimed to know anything about running a newspaper, they saw a gold mine in their new venture. "It's a piddling little paper now," Tammen said, "but we'll wean it on tiger's milk," wrote Fowler, a onetime *Denver Post* reporter.

Bonfils was convinced that the best news was local news: "A dog-fight on 16th Street is a better story than a war in Timbuctu." That philosophy forged a sensational brand of raucous tabloid journalism that fascinated and startled Denver. "Scandals were exploited to the hilt, and there was a crucifixion of a public official or non-advertising businessman in each new edition," wrote Robert L. Perkin in *The First 100 Years: An Informal History of Denver and the* Rocky Mountain News. "Everyone damned *The Post*—and nearly everyone subscribed." Hosokawa added that "in a rough, uninhibited time in a frontier city, the pair used their newspaper to assail their enemies and further their not always modest ambitions."

F.G. "was our most dramatic citizen," wrote Thomas Hornsby Ferril in *The Rocky Mountain Herald*. "Denver was his theater, the blue sky his proscenium, and *The Post* his workshop. Our citizens were his actors, villains, crooks, heroes, sinners, saints; sometimes they were puppets not knowing the plot and what strings Fred Bonfils was pulling." Ferril recalled an incident that measured Bonfils's reputation: "Tom O'Donnell, the famed, old fire-eating lawyer at the turn of the century was charged with being a friend of Bonfils. Tom assumed a

Demosthenes-like pose and spoke out loud and clear: 'A friend of the proprietor of *The Denver Post*? I'd rather be a friend of the rat that breeds bubonic plague in the foul miasmas of the sewer.'"[5]

Big-city newspapers also condemned the *Post* as a travesty of journalism, but Bonfils and Tammen's aggressive tactics—sensationalism, sentimentality, and slapstick—proved it paid to be noisy. By 1901 the *Post* had exceeded the paid circulation of Denver's first newspaper, the *Rocky Mountain News*. The *Post* continued to build up its advantage and then held it for decades. Bonfils and Tammen grew wealthy together. By 1908 each took a salary of $1,000 a week and split stock dividends that amounted to more than $1 million a year. For these two men it really was "a privilege to live in Colorado," and that slogan, which Bonfils wrote, remains on the *Post*'s masthead.

"There is no hope for the satisfied man" was another Bonfils slogan. He pushed himself to excel, expecting his *Post* staffers and family to follow his rigorous example of hard work and plain living, and tolerated no defiance. Belle, his quiet, uncomplaining wife, stayed in the background, apparently resigned to her husband's unyielding regimen. Meanwhile, Helen had learned early the art of diplomacy in dealing with her father, but for May diplomacy was as foreign a concept as Timbuctu was to her father.

Each evening Bonfils read every item in the *Post* to prepare for the next morning's postmortem with his staff. By 9 P.M. he was ready to go to bed and expected everyone else to retire as well. May tolerated the house rules while she was a schoolgirl at Denver's exclusive Wolcott School for Girls and St. Mary's Academy, but when she entered the fashionable Brownell School for Girls in New York, she enjoyed her first taste of intoxicating freedom.

F.G.'s favorite daughter had grown into a shapely, five-foot-two, beautiful young woman, a painfully obvious reality that worried her possessive father. By 1904 her brilliant blue eyes and blond hair attracted suitors by the score. Bonfils severely discouraged them, certain that all of them were only after her wealth. On a visit home in her senior year at Brownell, May told Bonfils that she was going to a dance to celebrate her birthday. He said she should celebrate it at home with her family. "You don't love me, or else you wouldn't want to go out tonight."

"But, Papa," she protested, "I'm 21 years old now."[6]

A younger May Bonfils. (Western History Department, Denver Public Library)

Bonfils insisted that she could go only if he accompanied her. May went to the party escorted by her father, a humiliating experience that she resolved would never happen again. Although May appeared to epitomize a demure young woman, her beauty masked the headstrong Bonfils gene.

The future heiress found salvation in one of stodgy Denver's conventions. At the turn of the twentieth century, young women from wealthy families lived at home until they married. May used the custom to her advantage and married the first eligible man who asked her. The hapless suitor was Clyde V. Berryman, a twenty-three-year-old sheet music and piano salesman who clerked in a downtown Denver music store. F.G. did not see anything good in him, while May saw emancipation in the man she had only recently met.

In November 1904, while Bonfils was out of town, the young couple eloped to Golden and were married in a civil ceremony. Bonfils was furious when he found out, but there was nothing he could do except refuse to send May her clothes. Neither her parents nor the Roman Catholic Church acknowledged the marriage. "In time F.G. would transfer his love to his other daughter, no less headstrong than May but prudent enough to play the 'papa's girl' role."[7] F.G. sent May affectionate letters, but the two never regained a close relationship. He could not accept his son-in-law, and May would not apologize.

During the next dozen years May and Clyde lived in Omaha, Kansas City, and Wichita, where Berryman ran a music store subsidized by his father-in-law. After eight years Bonfils withdrew his support , and the business failed. The couple moved to California, where Belle and Helen frequently visited the Berrymans. Clyde seemed incapable of earning a living.

May and Clyde returned to Denver around 1916 and lived at 1129 Lafayette Street in a four-bedroom house that F.G. bought for May from Walter Cheesman, the Denver railroad builder and real estate developer. The childless couple led separate lives there. May, supported by her mother, frequently traveled to Europe during those years, collecting antiques and art objects to decorate her Denver Square home. Her husband would visit the *Post*, usually when Bonfils was not in his office. Old-time *Post* employees recalled that "Berryman was not particularly likeable."[8]

Twenty-nine years later, in 1933, F.G. was still so angry at May for marrying Berryman that he punished her from the grave. After his death, his estate was conservatively valued at $14 million, although his investments were so varied and extensive that it was likely that many of them did not appear on the estate inventory. Regardless, it was the largest ever probated in Colorado at the time. The Frederick G. Bonfils trust provided liberally for Belle and Helen, but not so liberally for May. Belle immediately protested her husband's will, which gave her only an annual income, and won her widow's option of 50 percent of F.G.'s entire estate. In the same will, F.G. inflicted on May his final fury: he stipulated that unless Clyde Berryman died or May divorced him, she would receive only half of her sister's annual income of $25,000. Livid at such injustice, May followed her mother's example and also contested the will. She contended that the provision limiting her benefits was "contrary to public policy and good morals" by encouraging a divorce and therefore was invalid. The court agreed with May, awarding her the full $25,000 annual income.

Belle died two years after her husband, leaving a $12 million estate and a will that again rewarded Helen and nearly broke May's heart. While Helen could bank her 50 percent legacy immediately, May would receive only the trust income from the other half of Belle's estate. Further, Belle named Helen as trustee, who thus signed May's checks from the trust—a cruel blow. Finally, all of F.G.'s *Denver Post* stock that Belle had sued for went to Helen, while May had only annual stock dividends from her mother's shares. Acutely sensitive to equity, May again called her lawyer, Edgar McComb, who filed a petition to set aside the will. His petition charged that Belle had been unsound in mind and body after F.G.'s death, that she had been under Helen's domination, and that Helen had persuaded her mother to sign a will favorable to her. During a raucous court hearing, the sisters screamed insults at each other. Newspaper circulation spiked as reporters covered the local dogfight. Helen was mortified; May was not.

Evidence presented privately over the matter of Helen's domination of her widowed mother apparently had merit. Though Mary Sharp Dunkin, May's goddaughter (the daughter of her best friend Minnie E. Sharp), did not participate in any official testimony, she recalled that "Auntie May" told "everything to my mother," including a trip that Belle and Helen had taken to Kansas City shortly after F.G.'s death in 1933. Belle told Auntie May that Helen's Kansas City lawyers had Belle sign all kinds of things. "I don't know what I signed," Belle cried.[9]

An anonymous letter sent to May during the 1935 battle over Belle's controversial will reads:

> May Dear: I have been intending to call you on account of the system prevailing at the *Post*—I have been afraid your sister would discharge me—but I wanted to let you know that you have my sympathy over the horrid way that Helen and Anne O'Neill [Bonfils's personal secretary] are trying to deprive you of what is really yours— It might not be so easy now. From what I hear there is a Mr. Jack Finnerty who for sometime was in the confidential employ of your father. Helen discovered some time ago that he is not for her but, in reality, has been assisting you and has gathered a great fund of information which she believes that he has turned over to you and is now worrying himself to death.
>
> She would like to fix it up with him and has a private detective watching him all the time.
>
> Now, May, all this I have received from one of Helen's closest friends and whether or not this information can help you or not, I don't know but, I feel that you have been so unjustly treated that if there is anything I could do to help you I would want to do it.
>
> May, dear, some day when this thing is all over I am going to tell you who this is. With lots of love and luck, Your Friend.[10]

McComb's petition to set aside Belle Bonfils's will succeeded. In December 1935 a compromise was approved by county judge George Lexford. The *Rocky Mountain News* reported the story: "Belle was unduly influenced and her mind was overcome when she set down provisions which May and attorney McComb objected to."[11] An out-of-court settlement divided Belle's assets, which, McComb said, were "split right down the middle and right out to the fourth decimal point." Wrote editor Gene Cervi, "Without McComb, May Bonfils would probably have died penniless."[12]

May and Helen were rich, "but no attorney at whatever the price possessed the human skills necessary to patch up the differences of two proud, willful women."[13] Helen, as executor of her parents' estates, head of the F.G. Bonfils Foundation, and through outright ownership, now held the most stock in the *Post* and had power over it. When she assumed control as secretary and treasurer of the newspaper, one of her first orders was that May's name never again appear in the *Post*'s business or society sections. Editors obeyed the unwritten rule, and May could do nothing except resent it. The two sisters never spoke to each other again.

May was never close to the newspaper, and now, although she shared in its profits, she played no role in management decisions and didn't vote her approximately 15 percent of *Post* stock. Between 1935 and 1948, her annual income from the *Post* averaged $212,000.[14] She never visited the printing plant. She was bitter in her protest against the management, the waste of overhead, and the giving of expensive parties. Cervi once asked her if she wanted to visit the *Post*. "I don't want anything from those burglars down there but my money," she cried in her high squeaky voice.[15]

Hosokawa writes that "May was making legitimate news from time to time, mainly from her charities." Loretto Heights College, a Catholic school for girls, was one she generously favored, and the nuns, who were ignorant of the sisters' feud, embarrassed *Post* writers on several occasions. Society editor Patricia Collins attended a luncheon at the college one day and found herself seated next to May, whom she recognized immediately because of her resemblance to Helen. After some small talk, May asked Miss Collins, "My dear, are you a teacher here?"

"No, ma'am," Collins replied.

"Well, are you a student here?"

"No, ma'am."

"Well, what do you do?" asked May.

"I'm the society editor for the *Denver Post*." That ended the conversation for the rest of the afternoon.[16]

The 1930s were terrible times for Colorado, which was suffering economically from the Great Depression and simmering on the western edge of the Dust Bowl. Relentless heat and parching winds threw topsoil into the sky in clouds that darkened Denver streets at midday.

But for May Bonfils these were the best of times. In 1934, Clyde Berryman had left her, and the relieved fifty-one-year-old saw splendid possibilities in her freedom. Berryman pressured her to get a divorce, but May was too busy. She had decided to build a new house. She already owned ten acres enclosing Kountze Lake in Jefferson County and then bought more than a square mile of land surrounding the original parcel. Her rolling high prairie land with an uninterrupted view of the Rocky Mountains demanded a home equal to its setting.

May hired J.J.B. Benedict, "one of the most flamboyant personalities in Denver's architectural history, who designed some of the city's grandest Beaux Arts residences and churches."[17] Notable among his many structures are the Holy Ghost Catholic Church at Nineteenth

Belmar's front entrance faced east and featured lavishly landscaped grounds, larger-than-life statuary, herds of fallow deer, and flocks of peacocks and swans. (Western History Department, Denver Public Library)

and California Streets, the George Cranmer home at 200 Cherry Street, and the chapel at St. Thomas Seminary. In 1939 the *Architectural Record* listed Benedict's design of Belmar as one of the ten best buildings in the Denver area.

The home's two-story front entrance, at the end of a long, tree-lined driveway, faced east. High walls surrounded the property, constantly patrolled by armed guards. The lavishly landscaped grounds housed a herd of fifty fallow deer, peacocks, swans floating on Kountze Lake, and oversized statuary. In 1939, May added a historical building, a log structure she believed to have been built by Count Henry Murat in 1851 as the Hotel El Dorado at 1249 Tenth Street. Denver's oldest remaining structure, which had flown the first American flag in Colorado Territory, was scheduled for demolition. May bought the relic and had it moved to Belmar, where it stood near barns and stables housing her livestock: Suffolk sheep, milk cows, and chickens.[18]

Belmar's twenty-two rooms included an art salon, a dining room paneled in walnut, "and everywhere there were rococo French furnishings, silver, china, and tapestries," observed writer Marjorie Barrett in the *News*.[19] Belmar also had a small chapel off the foyer where May could pray, meditate, and attend daily mass conducted by priests from St. Elizabeth's Catholic Church in Denver. A solarium facing west overlooked a tiered marble fountain, the same one now visible at the pocket park on Speer Blvd. in Denver. Beyond Belmar, miles of open land stretched west to the foothills and the mountains.

The Belmar library was the house museum, filled with replicas of famous statues May had seen in visits to the Louvre, the Prado, and the Vatican Museum. "A giant table and cabinet designed by the famed French furniture craftsman Charles Antoine Boulle were originals from Versailles Palace. The room's walls were hung with several masterpieces—a Correggio, a Van Dyck, a Holbein called 'The Girl with Red Hair,' a portrait of Queen Elizabeth, and a Corot."[20] The Bonfils family obsession with Napoleon was passed down to May; a Chippendale case held the original silk gauntlet that Napoleon had worn when he was crowned emperor of France. May's love for anything Napoleonic stood out in crests on statuary, vases, furniture, and jewelry.

The mansion's west side faced Kountze Lake and the Rocky Mountains. The tiered marble fountain is now visible to the public in the Hungarian Freedom Park at Speer Boulevard and Emerson Street in Denver. (Western History Department, Denver Public Library)

The grand salon's walls were covered in bright pink damask silk bordered in gold frames. A treasury of items reputed to have come from Holyrood Palace in Edinburgh and St. James Palace in England were displayed. "A regal chair, the seat bearing the crest of Victoria Regina, is the command seat from which she [May] commands her guests. It is the very chair in which Queen Victoria sat."[21]

In 1988, *Denver Post* columnist Jack Kisling asked veteran appraiser J. Robert Welch how much it would cost now to build and furnish Belmar. "Welch rolls his eyes in a way that conveys the answer, which lies somewhere between incalculable and inconceivable."

Although she lived lavishly, May invested much of her annual income from her 15 percent share of *Denver Post* stock into a blue-chip portfolio. Her fortune grew.[22] She also amassed a dazzling collection of jewels valued by Parke-Bernet Galleries in New York at more than $2 million.[23] Only a handful of her friends were allowed to view parts of her jewelry collection at her infrequent dinner parties. Welch remembered a diamond story that involved one of May's many pet dogs. At one Belmar party, May wrapped a diamond necklace around her poodle's neck to amuse her guests. As the dog raced up and down the halls in excitement, May yelled over the staircase to the servants downstairs, "Don't let the dog out!"[24]

Her jewelry collection was so large that after her death, two auctions were required to dispose of it, one at the Parke-Bernet Gallery and the other at Belmar. The local auction "took up a small room," according to Denverite E. Atwill Gilman, who added that all the precious stones had been removed from their settings because May did not want others to wear what she had worn. Parke-Bernet judged May's jewelry as one of the world's most important collections. Probably the most fantastic piece was a diamond pendant called The Idol's Eye. Set in platinum, the 70.2-carat diamond was surrounded by 35 carats of smaller diamonds that she bought in 1947 from the famed New York City jeweler Harry Winston. He became her personal friend and made frequent trips to Denver to show her jewelry. From Winston she also bought The Liberator, a diamond found in Venezuela and named in honor of Simón Bolívar. The Maharajah of Indore sold her a diamond and emerald necklace whose total weight was 153 carats.[25] Other cataloged items were a collection of the world's largest and most perfect pearls—one a graduated strand of ninety-five. Proceeds from the premier auction went to the US Air Force Academy Foundation, the May Bonfils Stanton Catholic Chapel at the Air Force Academy, the University of Colorado Medical School, the May Bonfils Stanton Clinics in Denver, and Seeing Eye Dogs for the Blind Association.

May led a reclusive life at Belmar and, according to Cervi, "was a lonely person." She persuaded her best friend, Minnie E. Sharp, and her family to move to Denver from Wichita, Kansas. Mary Sharp Dunkin said that "Auntie May and my mother talked on the telephone every day." When May visited the Sharp home in east Denver, a chauffeur sat outside in the car. The Sharps were grateful for the driver's presence because they worried that without him, May's jewelry might be stolen.[26]

The Dunkins were frequent guests at Belmar. Mary remembered that "May was a fine pianist" and entertained by playing her favorite Chopin pieces on the piano, whistling as she performed. She recalled that there was one thing no young guest could do: play with Auntie May's doll collection. "Nobody touched it," Mary said. "May had had enough of sister Helen ruining everything when she got into May's things as a child. There was such a huge age difference." As an adult, May sewed clothing for the dolls, dressing them daily. Her first, a giant rag doll, always lay on a tufted chaise lounge in May's bedroom.

May promised her goddaughter that she would leave everything to her when she died. "Then Auntie May started adding on requirements. One, to be eligible, I could never marry. I said 'To heck with that' and married anyway. Mary received $10,000 upon May's death.[27]

Unless she went to Europe to buy antiques for Belmar, May, who was not interested in Denver society or the *Denver Post*, preferred her own company. She kept meticulous accounts of her farm's chicken and sheep production, listing profits from the sale of eggs and wool and cash prizes won at county fairs. She opened her gardens to local Brownie and Girl Scout troops every summer and would appear at an upstairs window and wave regally to the campers. Later she donated ten acres of land on the east side of Wadsworth Boulevard as a day camp for the scouts.

Local residents perceived May as a benevolent character. Walter E. Ziegenbein, owner of the Lewis Drug Store at 8490 West Colfax Avenue in Lakewood, remembered that May "came in here almost every night for years. May always ordered cherry lemonade and had ice cream cones sent out to her chauffeur and dog waiting in the car. She often gave gifts of money to the girls at the fountain." Ruth Taylor, an employee, recalled that "May wore fantastic hats and plain white face powder. She used to love to go behind the counters and poke through drawers, looking for new cosmetics."[28]

In 1943, May finally divorced Berryman, who was living at 1637 Newport Street in Denver. She moved to Reno, Nevada, to establish residence and testified in court that "Berryman hadn't provided her with the common necessities of life, that her fear of him destroyed her health, and that there was no chance of reconciliation." May won the uncontested divorce. Four years later she filed for a second divorce from Berryman in Colorado, testifying that "Clyde hadn't given her a dime" since 1934. She was awarded another divorce and her maiden name was restored; May paid her ex-husband $200,000 for the favor.[29]

During her lifetime May's philanthropy was extensive, although the *Post* wouldn't report it. Major gifts to Loretto Heights College include its Bonfils library-auditorium. Decoration of the Air Force Academy Catholic Chapel with giant mosaic murals and Stations of the Cross were imported from Italy by Bonfils. She set up the May Bonfils Clinic of Ophthalmology at the University of Colorado Medical Center. She rebuilt and then endowed St. Elizabeth's Church and monastery on the Auraria Campus at 1060 11th Street. May also endowed the Villa Nazareth Orphanage in Rome with a substantial sum. The Denver Art Museum displays her doll collection, old master paintings, and paintings by Amedeo Modigliani and Raoul Dufy in the Bonfils wing; the Denver Museum of Nature and Science and the Denver Public Library have Bonfils exhibition halls. After her death, personal bequests of money went to her friends, the Belmar staff, and for the care of any animals she owned at the time of her death.

Whenever May gave substantial sums to Colorado institutions, they needed an official biography to credit the obscure philanthropist. May was virtually unknown because she led a reclusive life and the *Post*, under orders from Helen, did not report about her or her philanthropy. Still, recipients needed her photograph. As she aged, May was "solidly built, ample-bosomed, shorter than her sister Helen, notice-

Marble statuary adorned the grounds. (Western History Department, Denver Public Library)

59

ably older, and slow walking."[30] May provided a photograph that showed a much younger, fashionable woman wearing furs, jewelry, and an elegant feathered hat designed by the House of Fontana in Rome, which created exclusive garments for her. May refused to update the photo, banning anyone from taking a new photograph of her. The press packet did not include May's birthdate or her final passport. Estate appraiser Welch found that passport and concluded that she had burned a hole in the document to delete her birthdate.

According to Cervi, May resented the publicity her sister Helen received in print, and she didn't hesitate to say so. She also resented that Helen used the *Post* as a vehicle of personal aggrandizement while banning May's name from the paper. She denied the decades-long alienation from her father, insisting that "I was Papa's girl." She complained that she, too, should be acknowledged in the significant gifts of money from the Frederick G. Bonfils Foundation, because she was also his daughter. "Helen has no right to hog the show. She had no right to build that theater [the Bonfils Theater at East Colfax Avenue and Elizabeth Street] for herself so she could show off her acting." May complained to Cervi that more than a few people had tried to effect a reconciliation between her and Helen, "But they don't know what it's all about and they should stop trying to butt in."[31] No one could be a friend to both May and Helen.

Among May's small circle of friends was a ruggedly handsome, six-foot-two-bachelor, Charles Edwin (Ed) Stanton. A third-generation Denverite, he moved to New York City where he worked as a designer for the Hilton Hotels and for Dorothy Draper, an internationally known interior designer. When Stanton returned to Denver, he headed the home furnishings department at the Daniels &Fisher department store. The couple met through the Central City Opera Festival. May had donated the garden linking the Teller House to the opera house and liked the work Stanton had done to upgrade and decorate opera association properties. The aging May asked Stanton to supervise an elevator installation at Belmar. The fifty-three-year-old man became a regular visitor.

May, at age seventy-two, shocked Stanton one day by offering him a job, "a lifetime job taking care of my things." She explained that she had accumulated a great deal of valuable real estate as well as other wealth, and since she had no children, she wanted Stanton to see that it would benefit worthy causes after her death. May was not looking for an ordinary business manager. Stanton's friend Welch added that May had said to the designer, "If you marry me and enable me to live at Belmar, I'll give you a million dollars. I want you to take care of me for the rest of my life. But you can't just live with me; we have to be married. In exchange for that, you have to pay for the groceries."

Stanton was dumbfounded. "I don't think that's possible," he answered. "For one thing, there's the matter of our ages."

"Don't say that again," May scolded. "I may be younger than you in my thinking. Your family is gone, and I have no one. Marriage would be the greatest thing in the world for me."[32] The bachelor eventually agreed to the idea, although May added conditions: Stanton could bring no furnishings from his own home and he must quit his career.[33]

The two planned to marry May 28, 1956, at Presentation Catholic Church. The night before the wedding, diocese authorities learned that May's first husband was still alive and quickly canceled the church's involvement. The couple married the next day anyway, at Belmar, with district judge Robert H. McWilliams officiating. May's nurse and Stanton's brother attended the pair, but there were no guests. One of Stanton's former girlfriends, socialite Eleanor Weckbaugh, heard the news and sent him a singing telegram: "So that's where you've been!" When Helen learned of the marriage, she had one brief comment: "That old fool."[34] May immediately transferred $1 million in bonds to the bridegroom.

It was a happy marriage that brought an end to May's seclusion. After first husband Clyde Berryman died in 1959, the Stantons went to St. Peter's in Rome to renew their marriage vows and receive the blessings of Pope John XXIII. The couple traveled to Europe often, entertained close friends at Belmar, bought a Rolls Royce, and decided to leave half of her estate in trust to the Order of Friars Minor's St. Elizabeth's Catholic Church in Denver.

Although May had insisted she would never sell her stock in the *Post*, at the end of her life she did. By doing so, she nearly destroyed the newspaper that not only served multiple generations of the Rocky Mountain West but also made her one of the nation's wealthiest women. In 1959, May was furious with the *Post* because it had either offended her sensibilities by not reporting that her Suffolk sheep had won grand prize at the state fair or by publishing a seven-paragraph obituary of her ex-husband that she felt was an "uncalled for airing of dirty laundry." Whatever the reason, May blamed sister Helen and Palmer Hoyt, editor and publisher of the *Post*. "This is the last straw. You are going to regret this story," she warned Hoyt in a telephone call.[35] May's decision was to punish them by selling all but fifteen shares of the 15 percent total *Post* stock she owned. In 1960, she sold the block for $3,533,765 to media king Samuel I. Newhouse, whose goal was eventually to gain control of the *Post*, just as he had gained control of the dozen newspapers he already owned. Newhouse's purchase was just the opening wedge in a years-long court battle that Helen fought in order to keep ownership of the newspaper in Denver.

When May announced that she had sold her *Post* stock, her decision rocked the foundations of the newspaper. The other owners of *Post* stock were local: the Harry H. Tammen Trust to Children's Hospital, the Agnes Reid Tammen Trust, the Frederick G. Bonfils Trust, the Bonfils Foundation, and Helen Bonfils Davis. (By now Helen was married to her second husband, Edward M. Davis.) May said her decision to sell to Newhouse was "based on carefully studied reports where Mr. Newhouse owns his many newspapers." Stanton agreed, noting the declining revenues of the newspaper due to management decisions to put money into the new physical plant at Fifteenth and California Streets, and intense competition from other news media. Bleak years of litigation followed. Ultimately, the *Denver Post* was sold to the Times-Mirror Co. of Los Angeles for $95 million.[36]

Selling her *Post* stock was May's final act of revenge against her sister. After a brief illness, she died in March 1962. She was buried at Fairmount Cemetery in a private Tudor-Gothic mausoleum that contains the altar from her Belmar chapel. When Helen was notified of her sister's death, she was a patient in St. Joseph's Hospital for various ailments, including diabetes and a weakened heart. Hosokawa wrote, "Without a change of expression on her proud, patrician face, she replied, 'There has been nothing between us for a long time.'" Helen did not attend the funeral.[37]

At May's death, estate lawyer W. Davis Moore asked Ed Stanton to come to his office. Moore informed the widower that May had rewritten her will, nullifying their prenuptial agreement. Stanton was

An aerial view gives perspective to Belmar's elegance.

astonished to learn that she had left the second half, $5.5 million, of her gross estate and Belmar with all its furnishings to him. He immediately formed in his wife's name the Bonfils-Stanton Foundation. It has offices in the Daniels & Fisher Tower, a Denver Historic Landmark. Upon his death in 1987, Stanton left much of his own fortune to the nonprofit. By 2003 the private foundation had total assets of $71,286,000 and had awarded more than $25 million in grants to Colorado institutions.[38]

Stanton lived at Belmar until 1971, developing the remaining hundreds of acres, part of which was the Villa Italia shopping center. By 1970, May's square mile was surrounded by ever-expanding Lakewood. Stanton donated land for the Lakewood Civic Center and some of the buildings for the Belmar Village Museum. He gave Belmar and ten acres of gardens on the estate to the Archdiocese of Denver to be used for the archbishop's residence and as a retreat. A year later the archdiocese sold the property for $350,000 to the Craddock Development Co. of Colorado Springs.[39] Martin H. Work, director of administration and planning for the archdiocese, explained that "the mansion's normal maintenance were $1000 monthly and that a year's effort to find appropriate use of the estate has been unsuccessful." One day after the property transfer to Craddock, demolition began on one of the West's architectural treasures. A generic shopping mall surrounded by asphalt parking lots has replaced Belmar and its gardens. Villa Italia was torn down in 1996 and has been replaced by mixed-use development. The Bonfils-Stanton Foundation leases all the land not otherwise given to institutions.

May Bonfils Stanton was a self-indulgent woman whose inherited wealth allowed her to live lavishly. She hired able lawyers, architects, and investment counselors. She loved Belmar, her second husband, freedom, animals, dolls, and cherry lemonade. She also loved Colorado and its people, a passion that dictated that every cent of her fortune must stay in Colorado through the Bonfils-Stanton Foundation and her church. Conversely, her epic feud with her sister Helen nearly destroyed a powerful newspaper that suffered reduced circulation, profits, and capital-draining lawsuits precipitated by her vindictive sale of *Post* stock.

May led a life of wealth, privilege, and unpublicized philanthropy, always following her own star despite the disapproval of her domineering father and estranged sister. She was one of the last of the state's colorful characters, a Jefferson County farmer who built a small palace, and idolized royalty, especially Great Britain's Queen Victoria. May's legacy, however, was one of generosity that continues to benefit thousands of Coloradans who frequently don't know how to pronounce her name.

Notes

1. "End of an Exciting Era, Start of Another," *The Sentinel*, March 15, 1962.
2. Bill Hosokawa, *Thunder in the Rockies: The Incredible* Denver Post, Morrow, 1976.
3. Ibid.
4. Thomas J. Noel, *Denver: Rocky Mountain Gold*, Continental Heritage Press, 1980.
5. Thomas Hornsby Ferril, "Ideas and Comment," *Rocky Mountain Herald*, August, 1953.
6. Hosokawa, *Thunder in the Rockies*.
7. Ibid.
8. Ibid.
9. Interview of Mary Sharp Dunkin by Marilyn Griggs Riley, September 8, 2002.
10. Bonfils-Stanton Papers, Box 3, Western History Department, Denver Public Library.
11. "Bonfils Will Contest Ends," *Rocky Mountain News*, December 20, 1935.
12. Gene Cervi, "I Was Papa's Girl," *Cervi's Business Journal*, April 10, 1966.
13. Hosokawa, *Thunder in the Rockies*.
14. Ibid.
15. Gene Cervi, "I Was Papa's Girl," *Cervi's Business Journal*, August 10, 1966.
16. Hosokawa, *Thunder in the Rockies*.

17. Thomas J. Noel and Barbara S. Norgren, *Denver: The City Beautiful and Its Architects, 1893–1941*, Historic Denver, Inc., 1987.
18. Display, Colorado Historical Society, 2004.
19. Marjorie Barrett, "Estate Sale Remnants of Belmar, Fabled Bonfils home will be sold Friday," *Rocky Mountain News*, February 27, 1988.
20. Pasquale Marronzino, "Mrs. May Bonfils Stanton Dies," *Rocky Mountain News*, March 13, 1962.
21. Ibid.
22. Hosokawa, *Thunder in the Rockies.*
23. Pasquale Marronzino, "$2 million May Bonfils Jewel Auction Set," *Rocky Mountain News*, October 28, 1962.
24. Interview of J. Robert Welch by Marilyn Griggs Riley, 2000.
25. Bonfils-Stanton Papers, Box 11, Western History Department, Denver Public Library.
26. Interview of Mary Sharp Dunkin by Marilyn Griggs Riley, August 2002.
27. Interview of Mary Sharp Dunkin by Marilyn Griggs Riley, August 2000.
28. *The Sentinel*, March 15, 1962.
29. Bonfils-Stanton Papers, Box 2, Western History Department, Denver Public Library.
30. Cervi, "I Was Papa's Girl."
31. Ibid.
32. Hosokawa, *Thunder in the Rockies.*
33. Interview of J. Robert Welch by Marilyn Griggs Riley, 2001.
34. Hosokawa, *Thunder in the Rockies.*
35. Ibid.
36. *The* Denver Post: *A Guide to 100 Years, 1892–1992*, Denver Post, 1992.
37. Hosokawa, *Thunder in the Rockies.*
38. Bonfils-Stanton Annual Report, 2001, Denver.
39. J. Robert Welch Papers, Box 1, Western History Department, Denver Public Library.

The Favored Daughter

Helen Gilmer Bonfils
(1889–1972)

Helen G. Bonfils, ultimately chairman of the board of the Denver Post, *benefactor, and Colorado's first lady of the theater, blossomed in mid-life after the death in 1933 of her powerful father, F.G. Bonfils, co-founder of the* Denver Post. *(Western History Department, Denver Public Library)*

"To know Denver history, one must know its rich families," observed John Clark Mitchell, II, banker and longtime fundraiser for the city's major cultural institutions. Mitchell mastered the chapter that starred Frederick Gilmer (F.G.) Bonfils (BON-feez), cofounder of the *Denver Post*, and his daughter, Helen. Their story is also the twentieth-century account of Denver and the *Denver Post*. "Helen was always generous, she always came through. Helen was vivacious, unusual, theatrical and spectacular like her father," Mitchell related.[1]

That two-generation phenomenon fascinated residents from 1895 to 1972. Early on, Denverites grew accustomed to exotic *Post* productions: waltzing elephants and tightrope walkers from the Sells-Floto Circus (which the *Post* owned) promoting the newspaper, Buffalo Bill handing coins to children in front of the *Post*'s building at 1544 Champa Street, and Harry Houdini struggling in a straitjacket while suspended upside down from the *Post*'s balcony. The *Post*'s excursion train to the Cheyenne, Wyoming, Frontier Days was an annual revelry from 1907 to 1970, and the newspaper's free summer operettas in Cheesman Park entertained thousands of Coloradans each July from 1934 to 1972. Helen's career as a successful theatrical producer and actress in Denver and New York City made national headlines. Meanwhile, F.G.'s two quarreling daughters, May and Helen, created their own news in bitter shouting matches in county court over opposing definitions of *fair* as applied to distribution of their mother's fortune. The Bonfils sisters also made what friends called "unlikely" (poor) marriages that became the talk of the town.

After her father's death in 1933, Helen began her own newspaper career as secretary/treasurer of the *Post* and also as president of the Frederick G. Bonfils Foundation. She was a soft touch for civic fundraisers, assuring them that their causes were identical to hers. For example, a prominent fundraiser for the University of Denver recalled that "Helen was tall, blonde, and gaily energetic—and though she loved acting on the New York stage above all, she was devoted to DU."[2] From 1936 to 1973, she gave nearly $11 million from the foundation to worthy causes. Her gifts included building the Holy Ghost Catholic Church in downtown Denver, the University of Colorado's Medical School Nurses' Home, the Bonfils Tumor Clinic, and the Belle Bonfils Blood Bank, named for her mother. She paid hundreds of thousands of dollars for college scholarships for young men and women. In one year alone, 1948, the foundation's gifts to churches of varying denominations amounted to nearly $1,400,300 and included organs to fourteen of them. The foundation's books show that $2,181,000 was spent to support symphony orchestras, the Denver Opera Foundation, and the *Denver Post* operettas. The Bonfils Theater at East Colfax Avenue and Elizabeth Street was another gift, and the Denver Community Chest/United Way received a check for at least $50,000 each year.[3]

Helen's gifts to individuals were also wide-ranging. Daily she received letters asking for small sums, and she would oblige. For example, when Sister Mary Anne of the Servants of Mary needed a communion outfit, the foundation wrote her a check for $15. For several years, Catholic high school girls who couldn't afford graduation dresses bought them courtesy of Helen's generosity. Unnamed recipients of gifts were friends of her parents: aging priests, nuns, and pastors of several faiths; Sells-Floto circus people; and former *Denver Post* employees. Helen built a church rectory at Mother of God Catholic Church at 475 Logan Street, for her spiritual counselor, Reverend Msgr. John V. Anderson. He was a lifelong friend whom she had met when he was a child sitting next to her in a church pew. Helen helped with mortgages for Henry Lowenstein after hiring him as stage manager of the Bonfils Theater and for Jack Gurtler's renovation of the Elitch Gardens Theater. Both debts were canceled at her death.[4]

In 1972 virtually all the gift-giving stopped. Denverites and Bonfils relatives asked in dismay, "What happened?" The answer was the creation of the Denver Center for the Performing Arts (DCPA). The Helen G. Bonfils Foundation and the Frederick G. Bonfils Foundation immediately ended their private charity status and diverted their total support to the future DCPA in lower downtown Denver. Before her death, Helen's personal lawyer and friend, Donald R. Seawell, had envisioned the ultimate gift that Helen could give Denver: a theater arts complex to be funded by her final will, later supplemented by a $6 million Denver bond issue and private donations. Seawell's vision became four square city blocks now consisting of a concert hall, theaters, an opera house, a parking garage, and administration offices, all tied together with glass-roofed gallerias for shops and restaurants. The two foundations Helen had controlled became "satellites" of the DCPA, with Seawell as chairman of the board from its inception.[5]

F.G. Bonfils, the source of both foundations, and Harry H. Tammen in 1895 cofounded the *Denver Post*, and its profits were the base of both men's vast wealth. "*The Denver Post* is Papa's monument," Helen said. "It is like he was, dynamic, protean and strong. I judge my life by my father's. I don't think mine has been much; I haven't done much or accomplished much. I'll always live in my father's shadow," she said.[6] Those who know of Helen's achievements would disagree with her modest self-perception.

Bonfils Theater manager Henry Lowenstein described Helen as "striking, not pretty. If you saw her, you didn't forget her. In her high-heeled shoes, she was nearly six-feet tall—regal and imposing"[7]

Helen G. Bonfils (Western History Department, Denver Public Library)

(Interview, 2003). She brought glamour to a provincial, pre–World War II Denver whose business and political leaders were content to maintain a comfortable status quo. That conservative mindset permeated Denver, even its fashion scene. Helen's couturier suits, luxurious furs, stilted high heels, and veiled hats contrasted sharply with the bland wardrobes of her contemporaries. Hope Curfman, the wife of one of Helen's personal physicians, described a city during the 1930s and 1940s that distrusted deviation from the norm. "Denver was hidebound then. Helen didn't wear corsets. She was slender, large-boned, trim, a woman with good carriage."[8] Denver society speculated about her age and gossiped that she certainly applied henna to her "bright" hair. Helen eventually gained a reputation of respect and affection from those "hidebound" first families through years of hard work and philanthropy. "She was really a sweet girl, as gracious then as she is now," one society leader observed, "but she did, the Lord knows, dress dramatically."[9] Still, many continued to believe that Helen, as generous as F.G. was tight-fisted, gave foundation money to soften her father's robber-baron reputation.

The younger daughter of Belle Barton and Frederick Gilmer Bonfils, Helen was born in 1889 in upstate New York. F.G. had moved his family there from Missouri to escape damaging publicity from a court conviction involving his fraudulent land scheme venture in Oklahoma Indian territory during the homesteading rush. By 1894 the Bonfils family had returned to Kansas, where F.G. was operating legal lotteries. A year later he pleaded guilty to violating the state's vagrancy laws by loitering around a lottery and gambling house "without visible means of support." He paid the fines and moved on to Denver.[10]

At the turn of the twentieth century, Denver had a population of 160,000 and was steadily emerging from its 1859 beginnings and the Silver Crash of 1893. Telegraph was the isolated city's major communication link to the outside world, and transcontinental railroads were turning an outpost into a transportation hub. Denver's 1889 Union Station building grew into a blocks-long structure, its steel tracks linking Denver to the Rocky Mountain West and beyond. Agriculture, mining, and service industries prospered. The city's population continued to grow with newcomers seeking a fresh start in a young state that had joined the Union in 1876. Other transplants were the "one-lunged army," as Denverites labeled the thousands of tuberculosis sufferers who came to the city's high, dry climate hoping to cure their illness. Cattle "barons" and mining "kings" without a drop of aristocracy in their veins moved down from the Rocky Mountains to the city's less rigorous climate. Those who could afford to lived in the fashionable Capitol Hill neighborhood, just east of downtown, which was filling up with an eclectic assortment of mansions. "Nobody who was anybody lived anywhere else," declared Capitol Hill resident and Colorado historian Caroline Bancroft.[11] The Bonfils family lived at 939 Corona Street near Bancroft's home.

In this young city, Tammen and Bonfils, both in their thirties, began a newspaper that made them rich. For $12,500 they bought the failing *Evening Post* and renamed it the *Denver Post*. Within two years the newspaper turned a profit. Tammen was jolly, blond, plump, resourceful under fire, and a showman. He owned a curio and souvenir store and published "The Great Divide," a flourishing mail-order catalog that sold "authentic" Indian artifacts made on-site by local schoolboys. In contrast, F.G. "was dark, leanly athletic, austere, a watch dog over his bankroll, a fierce and untiring worker, a man whose striking face portrayed, despite its practiced set of jaw, a vague unrest, a thirst, a bitterness, a frustration."[12]

"Within a decade or so," writes former *Post* editor Bill Hornby, "both men had been reviled by proper Denver, shot and grievously wounded in their offices, and were well known in the courts on matters of libel and assault." Bonfils, as editor and publisher, and Tammen, as business manager, were shaping a newspaper that "about half of Denver hated but all of Denver read." Lacking newspaper experience, Bonfils and Tammen were bound by no journalistic restraints. The result was an uninhibited type of journalism that shocked and often enraged the traditionalists. "The paper even looked different, with big type headlines in red ink on page one, altogether a gaudy *Denver Post* looking like an explosion in a type factory."[13] In 1907 the *Boulder Daily Camera* editorialized that "the truth is the *Post* is daily a disgrace to journalism."[14]

The *Post*'s owners were well-known through their brand of personal journalism that both entertained and enraged Coloradans. Its coverage of practical issues like farm and ranch production, drought, mining, and politics connected with readers' lives and sold newspapers throughout the Rocky Mountain West. One famous reader was Baby Doe Tabor. One day, Helen was driving her Pierce Arrow touring car and saw Baby Doe standing on a Denver street corner "dressed in nothing but rags," Donald R. Seawell recalled in a story Helen had told him. "Helen stopped immediately and asked, 'May I take you somewhere?' Baby Doe replied, 'Before I get in a person's car, I need to ask who are you?' Helen said, 'I'm Frederick G. Bonfils' daughter.' The old widow responded, 'Well, in that case, I'll get in.'"[15] Baby Doe later froze to death in 1935 in her husband's mining shack in Leadville, Colorado.

F.G. Bonfils, who understood the use of fear, ruled Denver by using it. For example, after the new Paramount Theater on Sixteenth Street opened, according to Denverite Jean Shepard, "Legend has it that the *Post* told the theater owners, 'Of course you'll advertise, or we'll say the new balcony is weak.'"[16] Aspiring politicians also didn't dare offend the *Post*. And the newspaper's investigative reporting on local concerns resulted in front-page attacks on prominent Denver leaders. One *Post* exposé of the privately owned Denver Union Water Co. showed photographs of water running over sewage and slaughterhouse sites before it flowed into Denver water mains. In 1914, Bonfils and the *Post* helped defeat the water company franchise when voters approved Moffat Tunnel bonds, establishing municipal control of the city's water system. "Whoopee! People Win!" exulted the headlines.[17] Another newspaper campaign focused on merchants who had refused to advertise in the *Post*, who became the target of a campaign against child labor employment in department stores. The newspaper dropped the campaign when store owners stopped hiring the underaged and began advertising in the *Post*.

Circulation and revenues continued to climb. By 1907 the net daily paid circulation was 83,000, more than the combined circulation of its three competitors. In 1908, Bonfils and Tammen began taking salaries of $1,000 a week and split stock dividends that amounted to more than $1 million a year, an annual bonanza that extended to the next generation of Bonfils and Tammen heirs. *Post* profits enabled the founders to multiply their fortunes through investments in the coal business, mining schemes, oil, and real estate.[18]

Meanwhile, Denver's Old Guard scorned the *Post* and excluded its owners from prestigious membership in the city's private clubs. In 1908, Mrs. Crawford Hill, leader of the Sacred 36, dictated Denver's first social register, her cross-referenced *Blue Book*, and cited the Bonfils family just once: in her roster of those "Worth Over a Million Dollars." Bonfils and Tammen admitted that they cared not a whit for the community's respect so long as it kept buying the paper. "Sure," Tammen conceded, "we're yellow, but we're read, and we're true blue."[19]

Tammen died in 1924; his half of the *Denver Post* stock, valued at $5 million, went to his widow, Agnes Reid Tammen, and to a trust for Children's Hospital. The Tammens had no direct heirs. Bonfils remained as publisher and editor of the *Post*, "The Paper with a Heart and a Soul," and by then the region's most powerful newspaper. It continued its huge red headlines printed on pink paper and its attacks on Bonfils's perennial foes: politicians, the "trusts," and "corporations." Bonfils died in 1933 at age seventy two. Local merchants and politicians attended his funeral "to make sure that he was dead and also buried deep."[20] Local columnist Gene Cervi later described Bonfils as "a man who left behind some good and much contention. Helen Bonfils has spent twenty-five years and huge sums to build a measure of good will towards the memory of him who ruled with a mailed fist that consistently clutched a gold-headed cane that concealed a gun."[21]

Taller than "Papa" and blond, Helen resembled him with the same bright blue eyes, prominent chin, proud carriage, and love for the theater. She grew up in a family that loved theater. "She liked to say she made her theatrical debut at a very early age when she rode an elephant in the grand entry at the Sells-Floto circus," wrote Hosokawa in his account of the *Post*.[22] Her paternal grandmother often took Helen to the old Tabor Grand Opera House at Sixteenth and Curtis Streets in Denver for matinee performances featuring leading stars of the day. "An old friend commented that '[Helen] almost grew up at Elitch Gardens Theater. I think she saw almost every Saturday matinee.'"[23] As a high school student at the Wolcott School for Girls at East Fourteenth Avenue and Marion Street, Helen often went directly from school to matinees at the Denham Stock Co. theater downtown.

After graduation from the National Park Seminary, a finishing school for girls in Forest Glen, Maryland, Helen returned home to live with her parents for the next twenty-seven years. On Sundays, F.G.'s chauffeur, driving a Pierce Arrow open touring car with Colorado license plate number 1, would drop Helen off at the doors of the Immaculate Conception Cathedral on East Colfax Avenue. There she joined other prominent Denverites like Mrs. Margaret (Molly) Brown, who carried a walking stick adorned with a beribboned bouquet of fresh flowers. Cathedral ushers in morning coats and pearl-gray gloves greeted the large crowds of parishioners dressed in their Sunday best.

F.G. kept a protective watch over Helen, fearful that prospective beaux were just after her money. He limited her activities to acting in the Denver Civic Theater and volunteering at the Margery Reed Mayo Day Nursery. Long after she reached adulthood, Helen had a curfew of 10 P.M., after which F.G. locked the tall iron gates to their home. One woman recalled, "I never saw Helen at any of the big social events of the year. In the first place, no one liked old man Bonfils; in the second place, he wouldn't let a boy take Helen to the party if she had been invited; and in the third place, there was her chorus-girl appearance."[24]

In 1903, elder daughter May had rebelled against F.G.'s restrictions by eloping with Clyde V. Berryman, whom F.G. despised. May had been his "favorite" daughter until she ran off with Berryman. The angry father and defiant daughter never regained their close relationship, and gradually F.G. turned his devotion to Helen, who then became his favorite. She was as headstrong as May, but wiser and more prudent. Helen remained in his good graces, and whatever her private thoughts may have been, she maintained a "Papa's Girl" image. Only after her father's death did Helen reveal that she had her suitors call for her at May's nearby home.[25]

In about 1917, F.G., wife Belle, and Helen moved to a fifty-one-room mansion set on a half-city block at 1500 East Tenth Avenue bordering Cheesman Park. F.G. had purchased the structure and its furnishings from Leopold Guldman, owner of the Golden Eagle Department Store, in downtown Denver. Robert Stouffer, chauffeur and caretaker of the mansion, described the interior as "lavishly furnished and decorated with Napoleonic effects."[26] The home had an indoor swimming pool, a dance floor, a bowling alley, and a stage and theater. Circular marble stairs led to the second floor. "There were huge crystal chandeliers, 500 pounds each, and inlaid parquet floors and tapestries, not wallpaper, covered the walls. The dining room ceiling was covered with silver leaf."[27]

During Helen's years in the Bonfils home, she became actively involved in her great love, the theater. At age forty, she organized the Denver Civic Theater with Miss Florence Martin, Mrs. Verner Z. Reed, and the cooperation of the University of Denver. Their intent was to provide audiences with good theater, gifted amateur actors, and professional direction. Housed in the auditorium of Margery Reed Hall on the DU campus, the three women underwrote most of the costs of production. The *Post* promoted the theater in its drama and society pages, and Helen, by her own guess, played more than 100 roles at the theater. Many of them were character parts because she was of an age best suited for them. In a comedy titled *Noah's Ark*, Helen played a cow, standing upright wearing a white-cow-with-brown-spots costume. "She took great delight in her monstrous udder which swayed between her knees," Bill Martin, a student stagehand, recalled.[28] Her evocative portrayal of the prostitute Sadie Thompson in Somerset Maugham's *Rain* stunned audiences that were unprepared for Helen's moving characterization.

One popular local actress was Mollie Lee Beresford, who starred in a production where "Helen played my maid and put black make-up on that porcelain complexion of hers. She wanted to do the very best she could. She was dedicated and always knew her lines. She always downplayed herself to others. She was very aware of others' needs and never claimed privilege in the theater group. No one *ever* called her Miss Helen in the theater like they did everywhere else," Beresford emphasized.[29]

Helen enjoyed her wealth. "Helen dripped with furs. She liked what money could bring for her own gratification and joy for other people. For example, one day during the Depression, she was at Neusteter's Department Store on Sixteenth Street, and I was there too. Helen wanted to buy a purse, and the clerk recommended her own favorite. 'Oh, my dear, a big cow like me can't carry a little purse like that,' Helen said. Then she secretly arranged for the clerk to have her 'favorite' purse."[30] Around the same time, Gene Fowler, a former

Post reporter, wrote *Timber Line*, an amusing mixture of fact, legend, and rumor that depicted F.G. Bonfils as a swaggering buccaneer of the Fourth Estate. Fowler's hilarious portrayal of her father infuriated the ever-loyal Helen. Once, while shopping for books at the Kendrick-Bellamy stationery and bookstore at Sixteenth and Stout Streets, she asked clerk Jean Shepard to recommend a best-seller. Shepard suggested Fowler's book, which so angered Helen that she stomped out of the store. Shepard was afraid she would lose her job; however, the next day Helen's chauffeur delivered a corsage and a personal note of apology to the anxious employee.[31]

At home Helen absorbed a good deal of the world of business by listening to F.G. talk about the *Post* and his investments in the Betterment of Mankind (BOMA) Investment Co., a family-owned holding company that was also the repository for his stock in the *Post*. Without a son to carry on the business of the newspaper, F.G. persuaded his nephew, Fred Walker, to change his surname to Bonfils. A 1916 graduate of the US Military Academy, Walker was in the same class as future president of the United States Dwight D. Eisenhower. He served in combat during World War I, and after the Armistice earned a graduate degree in engineering from the Massachusetts Institute of Technology. Despite his rank of major and a promising career, in 1924 he resigned from the army to join his uncle at the *Post*.

Helen wondered if her cousin's name change was part of a promise to Major Bonfils that he would eventually control the newspaper. Seawell, her attorney and successor as chairman of the board of the *Post*, recalled, "Helen told me that she marched straight to her father's office and demanded to see his will: 'You're going to show it to me.' F.G. did. 'I like your spunk. You're right about the will. I'm going to tear it up,' he said."[32] Helen, not the major, joined the board of directors in 1933 when F.G. died.

F.G.'s estate was valued at $14 million, a conservative estimate, but the largest ever probated in Colorado at the time. His widow, Belle, and Helen were the principal beneficiaries of F.G.'s trust; Helen was also named director of the Frederick G. Bonfils Foundation. Through separate claims Belle and daughter May broke F.G.'s will. Belle won as much actual *Post* stock as the widow was entitled to rather than receiving just the interest earned from the stock that was locked up in the foundation. The county court then awarded May the same trust income as Helen, $25,000 per year, not the $12,000 that May had been allocated by F.G., who had carried to the grave his grudge against her for eloping with a piano salesman.

Belle Bonfils died in 1935, leaving an estate valued at $10 million, consisting mostly of stock in the *Post*. As a result, Helen, now head of the F.G. Bonfils Foundation, and through outright ownership of her own stock plus 50 percent of her mother's, controlled nearly half of all *Post* stock. Belle's will, like her husband's, favored Helen, age forty-six, over May, age fifty-two. The favored daughter had inherited the Humboldt Street mansion and all of her mother's other personal property. In contrast, May was given just the interest on her 50 percent share of Belle's stock portfolio. Again, May sued for parity. A two-day hearing resulted in a shouting match over accumulated family grievances that made the headlines in Denver newspapers. Molly Beresford believed that the ugly public display had more to do with hurt feelings caused by flagrant family favoritism than with money. May privately threatened that if she didn't get her stock outright, she would bring charges that their mother had been mentally ill.[33] The heirs then agreed to a contract of compromise and settlement which provided that each woman would receive seven-sixteenths of Belle's estate outright, with one-sixteenth to be placed in a Denver bank for May's benefit and one-sixteenth in a Kansas bank for Helen. "The county court compromise could do nothing to ease the rancor between the sisters, and they went their separate ways, their paths never crossing except by accident," Hosokawa wrote in *Thunder in the Rockies*.

Helen entrusted the *Post* to her inherited managers; she was never a working employee, but rather a benevolent overseer, determined to keep "Papa's Paper" the same as when he was alive. She attended to her own affairs, and freed from restrictions, began a new life as an independent woman. Although she married twice, *Post* employees from the editor on down called her "Miss Helen." She became a strong leader who operated with a tough resolve whenever the newspaper was threatened. Ultimately, Helen became chairman of the board of the *Post*.

"Helen was one of those 'poor little rich girls,' an awful cliche," said Sheila Bisenius, Helen's goddaughter and the daughter of Anne Sullivan, F.G. and Helen's secretary. "Helen had dramatic talent, nowhere to prove it and was always criticized for being F.G.'s daughter. She was not a sophisticated woman. Ordinary people bored her, and she was uncomfortable with them. She wasn't Junior League material, and she didn't smoke or drink. Helen was dramatic, rarely off-stage and I didn't know who she really was. Her friends were a little bit extraordinary, off-beat. She had a lot of grandeur and glory, but remained small town in her humility—a strange mixture. She gave mixed signals as both Daddy's girl and worldly, which she was not."[34]

"Helen Bonfils is not easily explained," wrote Gene Cervi. "Nobody is. Especially the deserving, underprivileged, disadvantaged rich. Helen is all of these. No man ever was able to measure up to her father. She was told wrongly when she was young that money can do anything. Whatever the hidden frights, fears and rejections that came to Helen, she has made for herself an exterior facet of poise and dignity that wears well. The roses go to her."[35]

In 1934, Helen's old grammar school friend Arnold B. Gurtler, president of the Elitch Gardens Co., persuaded her to join the stock company at Denver's famous Elitch Theater, "one of the cradles of American drama," as described by Hollywood producer Cecil B. DeMille.[36] A dozen women tried out for the part of an Italian woman in *Men in White*, but Helen, who was basically shy, won the role, chosen by the director who had not been told who Helen was. "I wasn't nervous at all. It wasn't like playing oneself," Helen said.[37] She was a commanding presence, a tall, blond woman with a husky voice who was frequently compared to her good friend, Broadway actress Tallulah Bankhead.

Helen continued to play bit parts at Elitch's in the summers while working at the Denver Civic Theater during the winters. At Elitch's in 1936 she met and fell in love with George Somnes, a successful New York director and producer who had come to act in and direct the theater's productions. Friends remarked that Somnes greatly resembled F.G. Robert Stouffer, F.G.'s chauffeur, who stayed on to work for Helen, recalled that she told him, "I have never seen a man like that. He has such piercing eyes." One summer afternoon she offered to give Somnes a ride back to his rooms at the Brown Palace Hotel, a trip that convinced Stouffer that Helen was seriously interested in the director. She directed Stouffer to drive around the block to drop Somnes off at the hotel curb, rather than making the easier stop across the street.[38] "I saw Helen Bonfils fall in love with Somnes at Elitch's," remembered Beresford. "Helen could marry because she was free of parental control. 'I should go slowly, but I don't,' she told me."

That summer Jack Gurtler wrote, "Helen played the head nurse in *The Man Who Came to Dinner*, and George Somnes played the cranky guest. Audiences roared when he'd call out from his wheelchair, 'Miss Bed Pan, come in here and help me.' That was how the script read, but it struck Denverites very funny to hear the owner of the *Post* addressed as 'Miss Bed Pan.'"[39] Helen and Somnes, both well into middle age, were married when the 1936 season closed. "George was absolutely wonderful for her," recalled Bisenius. "He was a cultivated English actor, smart, and truly devoted to her." The wedding was held at the Arnold B. Gurtler home at 4209 West Thirty-Eighth Avenue across from Elitch Gardens. Mrs. Harry Tam-

Helen G. Bonfils and George Somnes, a New York theater producer and director, are photographed in 1936 after their wedding at the Arnold B. Gurtler home across from Elitch Gardens at West Thirty-Eighth Avenue and Tennyson Street. Helen wears her first wedding present, a string of pearls given her by Mrs. Harry H. Tammen, widow of the Denver Post *co-founder. (Western History Department, Denver Public Library)*

men, widow of the newspaper's cofounder, hosted the wedding breakfast and gave Helen her first wedding present, a string of pearls of great value.[40]

In 1964, Helen became head of the Elitch Gardens Theater and abolished the resident companies to institute a new policy of bringing in "package" shows with big names from Broadway. "At every Wednesday matinee, Helen always sat in the same chair outside the theater, where patrons would pay their respects to Helen as if they were greeting royalty. Helen always felt it was her duty to do that," said Seawell.[41]

The newlyweds divided their time between Denver and New York City, where they formed the Bonfils & Somnes Producing Co. Backed financially by Helen, they became highly regarded theatrical producers on Broadway. The couple leased the Little Theater in New York City for the 1937–38 season, producing a number of successful plays, including *Sun Kissed*, starring George Colburn, *The Brown Danube*, and *Pastoral* in 1939. Helen continued her acting, appearing on Broadway in small roles under her stage name, Gertrude Barton. Another Bonfils & Somnes production was *The Greatest Show on Earth*, the story of the Ringling Bros. Circus. When it came to Manhattan, Helen was front and center, riding in a fanciful carriage pulled by magnificent horses with plumed headdresses in the grand circus parade down Fifth Avenue. "Helen held court wherever she was," said friend and fellow Denver Players Club member James R. Hartley.[42]

She was president of the Twelfth Night Club, a society of actors in New York City, and served on the board of the American National Theatre and Academy. "She was in her glory when she was around theater people," wrote Denver newspaperman Gene Amole. "They seemed to stimulate her—make her laugh and be happy."[43] Her twenty-year marriage to Somnes was perhaps the happiest period in Helen's life. They bought a luxurious condominium in River House at 435 East Fifty-Second Street, New York City, where the couple made it a point to entertain any friends from Denver.[44] Sheila Bisenius and her mother, Anne Sullivan, were frequent guests at the two-story home overlooking the East River. "It was filled with French period furniture, moire draperies in chartreuse and amethyst, and a marble staircase joined the two floors. There was nothing subtle about it, and there were dogs and cats galore" (Bisenius, Oral History, CHS).

Bonfils and Somnes returned to Denver in the summers, living quietly in the Humboldt Street mansion that was still listed in the telephone directory under F.G.'s name. "Miss Helen liked to keep up on town happenings, and it was up to Georgia Barber, *The Post* society editor, and myself to have something to report—the juicier the better," recalled Pat Collins, who succeeded Barber as society editor. "In those days a befurred and bejeweled Helen Bonfils swept through on a regular basis, 8:30 A.M. to 4:30 P.M., and she made at least one daily stop at the society section, her domain and one she ruled like an empress. The Women's Department was on the second floor, and Miss Helen decided the office lacked a certain pizzazz, so she sent down an enormous oriental rug from her home to cover the floor. Talking to Miss Helen could result in a certain amount of quaking, but I soon learned she had a marvelous sense of humor and was completely fair. Our friendship and intimacies about our own personal lives lasted, almost, until the day she died."[45] Another *Post* reporter, Eva Hodges, remembered Helen "always calling people 'Darling' or 'Honey' or 'Dear' in lieu of knowing their names."

In Denver, Helen attended to business from her office at the *Post* building and went to daily mass in the nearby Holy Ghost Catholic Church, which had moved in 1924 to a new, unfinished structure at 1900 California Street. The congregation worshipped in a basement under a temporary tar roof, and Helen had seen people faint there in the summer heat. In 1943 she funded the completion of the church, adding a pipe organ, a sound and lighting system, and the novelty of air conditioning. J.J.B. Benedict designed the Renaissance structure, which accommodates 800 people. A blond brick campanile, cream-colored terra-cotta trim, and a green Mediterranean tile roof mark its exterior. Inside, 300 tons of travertine marble from Salida, Colorado, were used for columns, piers, and walls. A coffered ceiling, pews of dark hardwood, an intricately handcarved pulpit, and an altar canopy adorn the sanctuary.[46] In the narthex, a framed portrait has a brass plate that identifies the benefactor: "Helen G. Bonfils built this Church of the Holy Ghost in memory of her parents, Mr. and Mrs. Frederick G. Bonfils. Cost of the Church, $1.2 million."

Helen Bonfils stands next to Archbishop Vehr (left) at the Holy Ghost Catholic Church, 1900 California Street, Denver, as they celebrate the completion of the church. Helen donated $1.2 million in 1943 to complete the unfinished basement structure where the congregation had worshipped for nine years. (Western History Department, Denver Public Library)

The *Post*'s content and appearance changed dramatically in 1946 when Helen hired Palmer Hoyt away from the Portland *Oregonian* to become the *Post*'s new editor and publisher. Helen agreed to Hoyt's three goals: to give the newspaper respectability, credibility, and vitality. He ordered a new nameplate for its front page: "The Voice of the Rocky Mountain Empire"; added an editorial page, the first in the *Post* since 1911; built a new physical plant at Fifteenth and California Streets; and, with the exception of Helen's 1935 order banning her sister May's name, ended "the blacklist" of the paper's enemies whose names had been banned. Hosokawa writes that "A B Hirschfeld, owner of a large commercial printing business, for some reason had gained *The Post*'s enmity. Hirschfeld, with tears streaming down his face, visited the new editor within days of beginning his new job. 'Mr. Hoyt! Mr. Hoyt!,' he wept in gratitude, 'you put my name in the paper!'"[47]

More changes followed. Black, Hispanic, and Japanese-American faces then appeared in the paper's Saturday feature recognizing outstanding service to the community. The pink color of the front and back pages ended, a new typography replaced the old, red ink no longer dripped all over page 1, and reporters were assigned to cover the Rocky Mountain West. National and international news coverage became important. The paper prospered as never before, with distribution extending to a dozen other states, including Wyoming, Kansas, Nebraska, New Mexico, Oklahoma, and Texas[48] (*Thunder in the Rockies*). Hoyt's revolution "vaulted *The Denver Post* from one of the most notorious to one of the most respected regional newspapers."[49]

In 1948, Helen sold the family home to the Conservative Baptist Theological Seminary and bought a Denver show home at 707 Washington Street designed by J.J.B. Benedict. The Beaux Arts villa with stucco and red-tiled roof is now condominiums. The Bonfils Cheesman Park mansion was demolished, and a high-rise condominium building now occupies a portion of the old site.

Helen replaced the small Civic Theater on the DU campus with the larger Bonfils Memorial Theater, dedicated to her parents, since "My dear," Helen said, "it was simply brutal to turn away an audience." She bought the corner lots at East Colfax Avenue and Elizabeth Street from Messiah Lutheran Church and hired architect John K. Monroe to design a 66,000-square-foot space for the most modern theater in the United States. During construction, Helen's health was failing; she was a diabetic and unable to visit the site. Somnes took photographs and gave her reports on its progress. Her health returned, and she and Somnes attended the theater's 1953 opening of *Green Grow the Lilacs*. The first-night audience, "furred and jewel-spangled, gave her a standing ovation."[50] Later renamed the Henry Lowenstein Theater, it closed in 1986. The former performing arts venue will become a retail center; only the building's exterior will be preserved.[51]

Rocky Mountain News drama reporter Frances Melrose covered the Bonfils Theater and recalled a production, Mary Coyle Chase's *Mrs. McThing*, in which Helen played a character role. "She was clumping around on spiked heels and I was scared to death she'd break a leg." Melrose remembered Helen as "kind and generous. Since the *Post* and the *News* were rivals, my boss told me to quit reviewing Bonfils

Helen Bonfils portrays the baby sitter, Mrs. Newby, in "Loretta Mason Potts" which opens on Monday. Children in the Mary Chase fantasy-comedy are Kathleen Chase, John Fanning, Ralph Aarons.

Mary Chase's Fantasy World

Helen Bonfils portrays a baby sitter, Mrs. Newby, at a Bonfils Theater performance of Mary Coyle Chase's *fantasy-comedy,* Loretta Mason Potts. *(Western History Department, Denver Public Library)*

Theater productions because of advertising rivalry. I told Helen I wouldn't be writing about productions anymore. 'Oh, my dear,' said Helen, 'that's perfectly all right, but I don't want you to stop seeing the shows. I'll mail you a season pass.' And she did, but I couldn't use it."[52]

Helen's fur coats, jewels, silver, furniture, and rugs appeared in more scenes than she did. Jonathan Parker, father of prominent dancer and producer Cleo Parker Robinson, was Helen's stage manager. He would often visit Helen on mornings before new shows opened to get furnishings for the sets. "She would say, 'You're just in time to have some hot cinnamon rolls and coffee. What do you need for the sets? Just go upstairs and get what you need, but not until you finish the food.'"53

In 1956, Helen hired Henry Lowenstein as designer of sets and costumes for the Bonfils Theater. He had recently attained a Master of Fine Arts degree at Yale University and was looking for work. Lowenstein had never heard of Helen Bonfils, but was certainly interested when she telephoned him about the job at Bonfils Theater. The interview took place at River House in New York City. A footman at the front door greeted the young man and a butler ushered him inside. The two-story living room dazzled Lowenstein, who marveled that "you couldn't see the ceiling for all the chandeliers." Helen introduced him to another guest, a red-haired lawyer she had just hired, Donald R. Seawell.

"She was so nice to us," Lowenstein said. "She had pizzazz, she was charming, very intelligent, gracious. She didn't give a damn about Denver society and its parochialism. She laughed at it. And she was egalitarian."54 Jonathan Parker would agree. "She was a grand lady to allow me to work at the Bonfils Theater, because I was the first black stagehand in Denver." In 1959, Lowenstein had asked Helen to approve his hiring of Parker. "If he's a good worker, of course it's all right to hire him," she answered. Lowenstein added that despite some local criticism of Helen's decision, "That's the way it was."

"I owe Miss Bonfils a lot," Parker continued. "She never got all the credit she was due." Parker achieved another first, auditioning and winning acting roles at the theater. "People came from all over to see a black person on stage. I played all kinds of roles," he recalled. "In one of those roles, I played butler to Miss Bonfils's role as maid. She told me, 'Jonathan, you and I are going to make the best maid and butler ever on stage.'"

George Somnes died in 1956. Helen wrote to her friend Benjamin Draper: "I am going to NY and dread it. I can't describe the feeling I have about seeing the familiar places and the objects we shared so many years. I don't know what has become of my courage, Bennie darling, and my ability to face problems! I find I am sadly lacking these days in strength, both physical and mental."55

86

Helen, actress Haila Stoddard, and lawyer Donald R. Seawell in 1959 set up a corporation called Bonard Productions, which produced several dramas and musicals on Broadway and in London. Later, Helen and Seawell formed Bonfils-Seawell Enterprises and produced such hit shows as *A Thurber Carnival* in 1960, *The Hollow Crown*, *The Killing of Sister George*, and *Sleuth*, which won a 1971 Tony Award as best play of the season. They also produced the first US tour of the Royal Shakespeare Company. In the risky venture of theater production, Helen pioneered in lowering the cost of Broadway playgoing, providing at least 200 ninety-cent seats at performances of plays she produced.[56]

After Somnes died, "friends noticed that Helen seemed to be depending more and more on her chauffeur," wrote Hosokawa. The chauffeur was Edward Michael Davis, known as "Tiger Mike," whose wildcatting oil company Helen financed. "Helen was alone and frightened. She was vulnerable and had no social life. More suitable men were not willing to let her call the shots," said Sheila Bisenius, who added, "Helen needed companionship." Mike Davis had been a janitor at Shugre's Lounge in east Denver. After he quit the job, he came back one day to show off a new Cadillac. "I've found me a gold mine," he boasted. "I chauffeur for an old lady, and she likes me so much, she gave me this car."[57] Helen, sixty-nine, was nearly twice his age and six inches taller. She had frequent bouts of phlebitis, according to *Post* reporter Eva Hodges, and Davis often carried Helen to her car. She frequently felt that "no one loves me for myself. They only love me for my money."[58] Davis had, according to Seawell, "a third grade education. To get a passport, Helen's butler had to go with him to fill out the application." Nonetheless, "Haila Stoddard [her partner in Bonard Productions] said that 'Helen was apparently very much in love with Mike,'" reported Eva Hodges.

Davis pressed his opportunity, and in 1959 the two were married in New York. The event was reported in the *Post* a month later in a brief story, below the fold where it was less prominent, identifying Davis as "a Denver oil man." Bewildered Denver friends asked, "Who is Davis? Wasn't her chauffeur named Mike Davis? Could she have married *him*?" "Nobody understood the marriage. He was one of the cruelest people I ever saw, but he could smell oil wells," said Helen's personal physician, Dr. Frank McGlone.[59] Helen's best female friend, Anne Sullivan, was devastated by the marriage; her husband, John, maintained that Mike had drugged Helen into marrying him.[60] Soon after her marriage to Davis, Helen told Elmer Strain of the *Post*'s advertising department, "I just get so lonesome."[61]

Predictably, the marriage did not last. Helen's health deteriorated and she was in and out of St. Joseph Hospital for the rest of her life. Meanwhile, Davis, subsidized by Helen, had made some productive oil strikes, but the couple quarreled often. "His forays into oil were interspersed with lengthy visits to Las Vegas," where he maintained a relationship with entertainer Phyllis Maguire of the Maguire Sisters singing trio. "Oh, Mike's young, honey," Hodges records Helen as saying. "He has to have some fun." McGlone described an early affection between the two, but equated Helen's second marriage to her fondness for stray dogs and cats. Then Davis began to talk about what he would do when he inherited the *Post*.

Friends, including Father John V. Anderson of Mother of God Catholic Church, urged her to divorce Davis. Overcoming religious scruples, in 1971 at age eighty-two, she filed for divorce in Denver District Court. She complained of mental cruelty by Davis and asked the court to compel him to account for "considerable sums of money she had lent to Davis" in his wildcatting business ventures. Davis contested the suit and hired expensive legal talent, including Stephen L. R. McNichols, former governor of Colorado, and the famed Melvin Belli of San Francisco. Seawell threatened Davis that if he didn't sign the divorce papers, he'd shame him with *Post* publicity.[62]

In December 1971, Helen's lawyer, Walter Predovich, succeeded in getting Davis to sign the divorce papers. Predovich immediately visited Helen at St. Joseph's Hospital to tell her the good news: "Well, Helen, by God, we got the job done." Predovich said she broke down and cried in happiness. "She never thought it was possible and thought she'd have to testify in court and be so embarrassed. She so regretted the marriage."[63] Her maiden name was restored. The divorce settlement included giving Davis an undisclosed amount of money, the Washington Street home, the River House condominium in New York City, forgiving all his debts, but allowing him no access to her *Post* stock. She gave all of that to the Helen G. Bonfils Foundation, which could dispose of it only to the *Denver Post* Employees Stock Trust (DPEST).

Lawsuits were a regular condition of Helen's varied and dramatic life. Indeed, she once told her good friend James Hartley, "If I didn't have a lawsuit going on, I wouldn't know what to do with my free time." Her divorce from Davis was minor in contrast to the other legal battles she faced in the last decade of her life. During that period, lawsuits challenged the core of Helen's belief that "Papa's Paper" must always be locally owned, and she demonstrated an icy resolve to maintain that status. She would spare no cost to win the battle over majority ownership of *Post* stock. Theater, church, and charities had always been important to her, but now her primary concern was the *Post* and its independence.

In 1960, publisher Samuel I. Newhouse had paid $3,533,765 to Helen's estranged sister, May Bonfils Stanton, for her 15 percent of *Post* stock. Newhouse wanted the *Post* as the "crowning jewel" of his diadem of newspapers, and he had $500 million available to use. The Newhouse threat was real: lush dividend streams to the May Bonfils Stanton, Tammen, and Children's Hospital trusts had been diverted in 1950 to pay for the new $6 million *Post* plant at Fifteenth and California Streets. May sold out, partly because she was still furious with Helen, and also because her stock dividends, which had averaged $212,000 annually between 1935 and 1948, had dwindled to an average of $80,310.[64] "Similar revenue withering was irritating the trusts and heirs to the Tammen half of the paper," writes Hornby.[65] Newspaper production costs had increased, competition from television and radio reduced profits, and new pension plans and other fringe benefits to employees covered by various labor contracts ate into net profit.

Trustees of *Post* stock were obligated to maximize income from assets and distribute them annually, dispersing net profits as quickly as they came in. During the 1930s and 1940s, nothing was put aside for future expansion or modernizing the aging physical plant built in 1907. E. Ray Campbell, vice president of the newspaper and executor of the Agnes Tammen estate, realized that the *Post*'s dividend policies would have to be changed, "that the directors would have to stop giving it away a bit at a time to some very wealthy heirs."[66]

Helen called in New York attorney Seawell to direct the upcoming Newhouse legal battles. She recognized a newspaper war when she saw one. "Before I knew it," said Seawell, "I had the job of saving the *Post* from Newhouse."[67] The takeover war that followed "was bitter and stretched out until the last legal battle. It cost Helen some $10 million personally in addition to large numbers of *Post* shares. *Post* managers were coping with creating a stock purchase plan aimed at eventual employee ownership, buying stock to keep it away from Newhouse and toward employees, in addition to deferring management decisions to the non-newspaper necessities of lawsuits and lawyers.[68]

Immediately after Newhouse had concluded his stock purchase from May Bonfils Stanton, he told the U.S. National Bank trust department that he would be interested in buying all of the Tammen-related stock. This would give Newhouse control of the paper, with 54.7 percent. Helen vowed that "under no circumstances will Mr. Newhouse ever become a member of the *Denver Post* board. If he wants to fight it out, I'm ready to meet him in court."[69]

Newhouse never got another share. In 1961, Seawell, at Helen's direction, had set up the *Denver Post* Employees Stock Trust to foil Newhouse, reward employees, and guarantee perpetual local ownership. Helen gave substantial stock to the DPEST and later established a foundation for her remaining stock to be sold only to the trust. *Post* management then "bought the first bloc of stock that had been left to Children's Hospital by Tammen just two days before Newhouse made a late but competing and higher offer, as with the next bloc held for Tammen heirs."[70]

Both stock purchases by the *Post* were contested in US District Court by Tammen heirs Helen Crabbs Rippey and her sons, plus Newhouse. The *Post* was allowed to keep the purchased shares, but Helen had to pay the Children's Hospital trust a surcharge to keep the price, $5,311,694, up to what Newhouse might have offered. In the second purchase the Tammen heirs contended that the trust department sold out for a relatively low figure, even though it knew that Newhouse was willing to pay more. The Rippey family sued, claiming that the bank's hasty action had breached its fiduciary responsibility and deprived them of several million dollars. They won their point.

The district court ordered that all the stock purchased had to go on public sale, and it looked as if Newhouse might prevail. In 1967, US District Court judge William E. Doyle ruled that Helen, who "has been an important and benevolent figure on the Denver scene," could keep the Tammen/Rippey stock by paying an additional $150 per share.[71] Including legal fees, the Tammen/Rippey deal cost Helen nearly $10 million.[72] Newhouse, believing that every newspaper had a price, appealed the court decision.

In 1973, after Helen's death, the Tenth US Circuit Court of Appeals dismissed all of Newhouse's charges and ruled that both the employee stock purchase plan and the quest to guarantee local ownership were legitimate. The long fight was finally over, and Newhouse sold back his stock a few years later, at a profit of $1.2 million, to the Bonfils foundations, which emerged with 91 percent of the *Denver Post* ownership, and the employee trust fund with about 9 percent. "By this time, Helen Bonfils was dead, Hoyt had retired and the road to perpetual local ownership looked nowhere near as smooth as they had dreamed."[73]

By 1970, Helen was a permanent resident at St. Joseph Hospital. The newspaper made several corporate changes: she became chairman of the board and secretary; Seawell, CEO of the *Post* since 1965, now replaced her as president and treasurer. In 1972, although Helen was dying, her sense of humor remained. Seawell visited her in the two-room, top-floor hospital suite where "she was lying on the bed, reading a book about Denver's famous madames. And she said, 'Don, if I had to do it all over again, I'd want to be a madame. I'd be the best madame, darling!'"

Helen G. Bonfils, eighty-three, died in St. Joseph Hospital June 6, 1972. Her funeral was held at the Holy Ghost Catholic Church and she was interred next to her parents and George Somnes in the stately Greek Revival–style Fairmount Memorial Mausoleum. There, a family who held the spotlight for eighty years occupies the grandest burial setting in all of Colorado: front and stage center. Theatrical lighting illuminates the proscenium and its marble walls appear to shimmer. The scene seems just right.

Denver Post board chairman Seawell, also president of the Helen G. Bonfils Foundation, which was combined with the F.G. Foundation in 1982, assumed complete control of Helen's estate. In the waning years of her life, her business affairs were handled by Seawell and *Post* secretary Earl Moore. Eleven relatives challenged her will, astonished that her remaining assets were merely $263,819. According to the final will, everything else went into the foundation trust.

Seawell responded to outraged philanthropies and disappointed Bonfils family members: "I had to decide to be Santa Claus to everyone or concentrate on one thing. In her will, Helen Bonfils never included any institution. She didn't cut anybody out. What had gone to institutions went to the Bonfils foundations. She just did it to get foundation perpetuity in support of it. The foundations were a satellite to the DCPA and legally, you couldn't put money anywhere else."[74] Seawell knew that Helen had dreamed of a professional theater downtown, but she had never envisioned a performing arts center. He had. "One of the last things she said was her regret at being unable to build a professional theater downtown." Seawell saw "a glaring need" for performing artists in Denver and added, "If it hadn't been for the DCPA being built when it was in downtown Denver, LoDo would be dead." DCPA president Lester Ward echoes Seawell's view: "The formation of the DCPA was the catalyst that revived the entire downtown area."[75]

As the 1970s progressed and the DCPA was under construction, the directors of the *Post*'s governing board began to think of selling the newspaper. Nationally, many local newspapers were becoming group-owned in order to survive, and there were convincing reasons for selling. First, the DPEST was growing too slowly to let it acquire majority ownership or to be able to raise expansion capital in the foreseeable future. From a start of 8 percent in 1961, the employees had achieved only 18 percent ownership by 1980. To keep the newspaper going, it needed substantially more capital. Many at the *Post* were beginning to realize that employee ownership was an impossible dream. Second, the Bonfils foundations were using their capital to build the new DCPA. While critics claimed that Seawell and the DCPA "bled *The Post* dry," the DCPA received only funds that were paid out in dividends. The newspaper's financial statements to the federal government show that no operating funds were diverted.[76] In 1980, Seawell asked *Post* employee stockholders if they wanted to sell, and they did. "The stock owners realized a 500–800 percent gain on their investment," Seawell asserted.[77]

Eight years after Helen's death, the *Denver Post* was sold to the Times Mirror Corporation for $95 million.[78] "Papa's spirit no longer directs the *Denver Post*," wrote Gene Amole of the *Rocky Mountain News* in 1980, "and neither does Miss Helen's. Too late and too bad." The *Denver Post* is now owned by the nonpublic Media News Group, which purchased it from Times Mirror. William Dean Singleton is chairman and publisher.

The DCPA complex covers twelve acres and physically is the largest in the nation, with "the largest initial endowment any center of performing arts ever had."[79] Private and corporate donations and the Scientific and Cultural Facilities District also support the center. Ticket sales make up 62 percent of revenue. Housed there are the Denver Center Theatre Company, the Denver Center Theatre Academy, the Buell Theatre, the Quigg Newton Auditorium, the Ellie Caulkins Opera House, the Boettcher Concert Hall, Denver Center Attractions, administrative offices, and a multitiered, covered parking garage. Because the DCPA is tax-exempt, the title was conveyed back to the City of Denver for a lease that runs to 2050 at $1 a year. The city owns and leases the other venues.[80]

Helen G. Bonfils was the recipient of countless honors and awards in her lifetime for service to the community, health, the arts, education, and religion. In 1957, Denver movie magnate Frank Ricketson presented her with a bouquet of flowers and the Central City Opera House Association's coveted Gold Chair Award at the conclusion of the final performance of *Separate Tables* at the opera house. "We call her the first lady of the theater in Colorado for her work with Central City, her inspiration, and her efforts in behalf of theater," Ricketson said. The modest recipient, wearing a flowered silk dress, veiled hat atop her "bright" hair, purple gloves, and four-inch high heels, thanked Ricketson and the standing-room-only audience. "I don't deserve all this acclaim," she commented. "But like all women, I like to get it."

Helen's roles as daughter, newspaper publisher, actress, producer, and benefactor succeeded because she kept each enterprise separate from the other. Her heavy responsibilities demanded that she maintain distinct barriers, but these self-imposed boundaries puzzled Denverites. Helen's spectacular style and dazzling persona certainly confused her contemporaries, who were astounded by her serious theatrical achievements. Bisenius isn't certain "who her godmother really was." Lowenstein remembers a humanitarian who built the Bonfils Theatre "for all who wanted to come, whether in evening clothes or work clothes."

No one, however, can doubt her total devotion to Coloradans, who came first in all her decisions. The only argument Lowenstein and Helen ever had concerned the cost of costumes for a 1967 *Denver Post* operetta in Cheesman Park. To save money, Lowenstein rented costumes from a New York firm rather than having them custom-made in Denver. When Helen found out, she was furious with him. "Don't you ever do that again. My money comes from Colorado. If I'm going to spend my money, I want it spent here and not in New York."

Historians seeking Helen's monument will find it far beyond the confines of the Fairmount Mausoleum. From an epic legal battle to keep the *Denver Post* home-owned to the landmark Holy Ghost Catholic Church; from the Central City Opera festival to the DCPA; from the University of Colorado Health Sciences Center to every major cultural institution in Denver; from children at the George Washington Carver Day Nursery to unnamed thousands of grateful adults, Coloradans are her heirs.

She waited until middle age to enter the starting gate in a race toward career achievement. She was much more than a little rich girl, and her accomplishments cancel her own humble perception of always "standing in my father's shadow."

Helen G. Bonfils was one spectacular late-starter.

Notes

1. Interview of John Clark Mitchell, II, by Marilyn Griggs Riley, 1999.
2. Farrington R. Carpenter, *Confessions of a Maverick: An Autobiography*, Colorado Historical Society, 1984.
3. Bill Hosokawa, *Thunder in the Rockies: The Incredible* Denver Post, Morrow, 1976.
4. Interview of Henry Lowenstein by Marilyn Griggs Riley, 2003.

5. Hosokawa, *Thunder in the Rockies.*
6. John E. Drewry, ed., *More Post Biographies: Articles of Enduring Interest About Famous Journalists and Journals and Other Subjects Journalistic,* University of Georgia Press, 1947.
7. Interview of Henry Lowenstein by Marilyn Griggs Riley, 2003.
8. Interview of Hope Curfman by Marilyn Griggs Riley, 2002.
9. Drewry, *More Post Biographies.*
10. William H. Hornby, *Voice of Empire: A Centennial Sketch of the* Denver Post, Colorado Historical Society, 1992.
11. Interview of Caroline Bancroft by Marilyn Griggs Riley, 1976.
12. Gene Fowler, *Timber Line: A Story of Bonfils and Tammen,* Crown Publishers, 1933.
13. Drewry, *More Post Biographies.*
14. Cary Stiff, "Helen G. Bonfils: 1889–1972," *The Unsatisfied Man,* June 1972.
15. Interview of Donald R. Seawell by Marilyn Griggs Riley, 2002.
16. Interview of Jean Shepard by Marilyn Griggs Riley, 2001.
17. Sponsored by the *Denver Post,* "The *Denver Post* Centennial: A Guide to 100 Years," The Denver Post, 1992.
18. Not cited, "Death in Denver," *Time,* May 1933.
19. Robert L. Perkin, *The First One Hundred Years: An Informal History of Denver and the* Rocky Mountain News, Doubleday, 1959.
20. Not cited, "Death in Denver," *Time,* May 1933.
21. Gene Cervi, "The Morning F. G. Bonfils Died," *Cervi's Business Journal,* January 7, 1958.
22. Bill Hosokawa, *Thunder in the Rockies.*
23. Not cited, "Helen G. Bonfils Dies," *Denver Post,* June 6, 1972.
24. Drewry, *More Post Biographies.*
25. Hosokawa, *Thunder in the Rockies.*
26. Robert Stouffer Memoirs, Colorado Historical Society.
27. Marjorie Barrett, "Doctors Seek to Buy Bonfils Mansion," *Rocky Mountain News,* January 29, 1948.
28. Interview of Bill Martin by Marilyn Griggs Riley, 2000.
29. Interview of Mollie Lee Beresford by Marilyn Griggs Riley, 2002.
30. Ibid.
31. Interview of Jean Shepard by Marilyn Griggs Riley, 1999.
32. Interview of Donald R. Seawell by Marilyn Griggs Riley, 2002.
33. Sheila Bisenius, Oral History, Colorado Historical Society.
34. Ibid.
35. Gene Cervi, "Roses in Type for Helen Bonfils," *Cervi's Business Journal,* February 22, 1967.

36. Jack Gurtler and Corinne Hunt, *The Elitch Garden Story: Memories of Jack Gurtler*, Rocky Mountain Writers Guild, 1982.
37. Drewry, *More Post Biographies*.
38. Hosokawa, *Thunder in the Rockies*.
39. Gurtler and Hunt, *The Elitch Garden Story*.
40. Not cited, "Champa Street's Lady," *Denver Post*, September 23, 1936.
41. Interview of Donald R. Seawall by Marilyn Griggs Riley, 2002.
42. Interview of James R. Hartley by Marilyn Griggs Riley, 2001.
43. Gene Amole, "Too late—too bad," *Rocky Mountain News*, August 7, 1980.
44. Interview of Lester Ward by Marilyn Griggs Riley, 2003.
45. Pat Collins, "Reminiscences of 31 Years of Parties and People," "Contemporary," *Denver Post*, December 25, 1983.
46. Thomas J. Noel, *Colorado Catholicism and the Archdiocese of Denver, 1857–1989*, University Press of Colorado, 1989.
47. Hosokawa, *Thunder in the Rockies*.
48. Ibid.
49. Hornby, *Voice of Empire*.
50. Not cited, "Helen Bonfils Dies," *Rocky Mountain News*, June 7, 1972.
51. John Moore, "Lowenstein Theater deal a bittersweet outcome," *Denver Post*, March 6, 2005.
52. Interview of Frances Melrose by Marilyn Griggs Riley, 2001.
53. Interview of Jonathan Parker by Marilyn Griggs Riley, 2002.
54. Interview of Henry Lowenstein, by Marilyn Griggs Riley, 2003.
55. Benjamin Draper Correspondence, Western History Department, Denver Public Library.
56. Hosokawa, *Thunder in the Rockies*.
57. Ibid.
58. "Helen Gilmer Bonfils" lecture, Eva Hodges, Denver Posse of the Westerners, January 1999.
59. Interview of Dr. Frank McGlone by Marilyn Griggs Riley, 2002.
60. Sheila Bisenius, Oral History, Colorado Historical Society.
61. Hosokawa, *Thunder in the Rockies*.
62. Interview of J. Robert Welch by Marilyn Griggs Riley, 2002.
63. Interview of Walter Predovich by Marilyn Griggs Riley, 2002.
64. Hosokawa, *Thunder in the Rockies*.
65. Hornby, *Voice of Empire*.
66. Ibid.
67. Hosokawa, *Thunder in the Rockies*.
68. Hornby, *Voice of Empire*.
69. Hosokawa, *Thunder in the Rockies*.

70. Hornby, *Voice of Empire*.
71. No author cited, "Helen G. Bonfils Dies," *Denver Post*, June 6, 1972.
72. Hosokawa, *Thunder in the Rockies*.
73. Hornby, *Voice of Empire*.
74. Interview of Donald R. Seawell by Marilyn Griggs Riley, 2002.
75. John Moore, "Cultured Shifts, Denver Center for the Performing Arts," *Denver Post*, April 11, 2004.
76. Hornby, *Voice of Empire*.
77. Interview of Donald R. Seawell by Marilyn Griggs Riley, 2002.
78. Hornby, *Voice of Empire*.
79. John Ashton, "The House that Seawell Built," *Westword*, October 26, 2002.
80. John Moore, "Cultured Shifts, Denver Center for the Performing Arts," *Denver Post*, April 11, 2004.

Sin, Gin, and Jasmine

Caroline Bancroft
(1900–1985)

Caroline takes a break from the road at a "libation station" during a 1949 jeep outing at Mammoth Gulch, Colorado. The controversial chronicler of the state's past claimed to know Colorado's back roads as well as anyone else of her time. (Colorado Historical Society)

Historians have typically conducted their research in quiet libraries, using the Dewey Decimal System and reading black print on white paper. Colorado historian Caroline Bancroft wasn't typical. Indeed, her approach to the research and writing of nearly two dozen booklets and two hardcover histories of Colorado so disturbed many academic and armchair historians that, years after her death in 1985, her name still provokes debate. Perhaps the only non-controversial issue about Caroline was the gift of her hard-won estate to the Western History Department of the Denver Public Library and the Colorado Historical Society.

Nearly everyone who knew this six-foot, 190-pound paradox has a Caroline story. Some recall her as a sour woman with no sense of humor, while others enjoyed her irreverent wit. Some remember her as an eccentric Denverite who wore orange braids entwined with paper flowers on top of her head. Admirers say she was short on diamonds but long on friends. Several Colorado historians condemn her self-appointed freedom to construe facts as she pleased and still call herself a historian, while others admire her ability to capture on paper the drama and spirit of the state's past. Aspiring writers are grateful for her generosity to them. To critic or colleague she responded, "Call me Caroline. It rhymes with sin, gin, or jasmine. Take your pick," wrote Sandra Dallas in Caroline's 1985 obituary in the *Denver Post*.

A new scrutiny of Caroline Bancroft reveals more than just the imperious personality that so eclipsed her contributions. She was the first to take the people and stories of Colorado and make them topics of popular booklets, which have sold nearly a million copies and continue to sell. And she did it without any real backing or financial help, just a will to write the stories of Colorado in an easy, bite-sized manner.

Dallas remembered Caroline as a woman who "did a great deal for Western history. She made it palatable. I suspect more people learned Colorado history from her two dozen Bancroft Booklets than anything the rest of us wrote. She actually supported herself with her writing, which is more than most Western writers can say."

As former Colorado Historical Society chief historian David F. Halaas said, "Caroline was—and is—a force in Colorado history."

Despite the impact and popularity of her work, no book has been written about Caroline. The Bancroft name, however, is fixed in the Colorado landscape. Mount Bancroft, in the Front Range of the Rocky Mountains, is named for her grandfather, and Lake Caroline lies beneath its 13,000-foot summit. Bancroft's home at 1081 Downing Street in Denver is listed in the National Register of Historic Places.

Professional and personal crises dogged this statuesque woman throughout most of her life. A case in point is her *True Story* magazine $3,000 commission in the Depression year of 1937 to write a five-part serial on Colorado's star-crossed Baby Doe Tabor.[1] Caroline expected an easy assignment because she knew the Historical Society had a collection of Baby Doe's papers. Further, she had met the reclusive widow in 1927 when Caroline's mining engineer father, an old friend of Baby Doe's, introduced his daughter to the rags-to-riches-to-rags legend. The three shared a jug of homemade Prohibition wine in Baby Doe's Leadville shack, Bancroft says, as she listened halfheartedly to mining talk. As she later wrote in *Silver Queen: The Fabulous Story of Baby Doe Tabor*, she remembered a "little woman, very withered and unattractively dressed in men's corduroy trousers and a soiled, torn blouse."

Bancroft told Frances Melrose of the *Rocky Mountain News* that she faced unexpected difficulties in finding enough Tabor material to write the serial: "What I didn't know at the time was that Edgar C. McMechen, curator of the State Historical Society Museum, had been appointed executor of the Tabor estate and was in complete control of all Tabor material. He refused to release anything to me. The result was that instead of being an easy job, it became a very hard one." Although she scoured the state's libraries and courts of record and interviewed scores of old-timers, she needed still more information on Baby Doe.

Baby Doe was the young and beautiful divorcee who, in 1883, had married the famed silver tycoon, Horace A. W. Tabor, then the richest man in Colorado. Tabor lost his fortune in the Silver Crash of 1893 and died in Denver six years later, leaving Baby Doe nearly penniless. The widow returned to Leadville—10,152 feet above sea level—where she lived at her husband's abandoned Matchless Mine.

Baby Doe froze to death in the mining shack in the winter of 1935, ending the long vigil she had kept there since her husband's death.

Nearly as discouraging as McMechen's angry refusal to share was *True Story*'s editorial requirement that she locate an actual acquaintance of Baby Doe in order to fulfill the magazine's need for a first-person story. Bancroft began a search for people who had known Baby Doe. She finally learned that "Baby's best friend at the end of her life was a girl known as Sue Bonnie but whose real name was Naomi Poitiers. I went to State Street where the 'girls' were in Leadville, and found a girl who located Sue Bonnie for me. She was the one who had found Baby Doe frozen to death in her cabin. At that time, Sue Bonnie had picked up a couple of Baby's diaries. I was able to get these and I interviewed Sue at length. She gave permission for her name to appear on the articles as a writer, and she received $50 for it."

Then Caroline found Baby Doe's younger brother, Phil McCourt, an elderly pensioner living at the Windsor Hotel in Denver. McCourt was a crusty, embittered man who despised reporters, Melrose wrote. Only when a fellow pensioner commented that Caroline looked like Jenny Rogers, one of the two most celebrated madames in Denver's red-light district, did McCourt give her information she didn't have. (Years later, Caroline wrote *Six Racy Madames*, in which Jenny was one of the stars.) Finally, Caroline had enough material. She finished the serial, determined to write a more extensive telling of Baby Doe's life provided she could find more information on the Tabors.

In the late 1940s she returned to Baby Doe. As Caroline related the saga, her old nemesis, Edgar McMechen, lay dying "in the hospital, and I started putting on pressure to get Baby Doe's papers which were at his home." Bancroft believed that Tabor photographs, diaries, letters, and other irreplaceable artifacts were in imminent danger. According to Bancroft, she besieged three of the state's most powerful men for help: "I got Palmer Hoyt, publisher of the *Denver Post*, James Grafton Rogers, curator of the Colorado Historical Society then, and Duke Dunbar, Colorado attorney general, all to help with the pressure. We finally got the papers from Mrs. McMechen. We got them just in the nick of time."

Whether or not the rescue of the Tabor papers was as dramatic as Bancroft recounts, she used the collection to supplement her Tabor research and wrote her best-selling booklet, the eighty-page *Silver Queen*. Published in 1950, the first edition sold out at a dollar per copy. Twenty-two reprintings have followed, and the book remains in print. The priceless Tabor files, some labeled "Burn," as well as Baby Doe's diaries and scrapbooks, which Sue Bonnie gave to Bancroft, are secure and available for public use at the Historical Society and library. According to Bancroft, the rescue of the Tabor materials led to her lifelong passion to salvage what others didn't notice or value and then donate it to the institutions that safeguard Colorado history.

Silver Queen is a story based on history. With her breezy writing, Bancroft targeted tourists, recognizing their interest in Colorado history "before anyone else did," in the words of Colorado historian Louisa Ward Arps. Each Bancroft Booklet is easy to read and contains vintage photographs. The post–World War II readers who bought Bancroft's histories also read western novels, vacationed on dude ranches, enjoyed western movies, and watched television programs

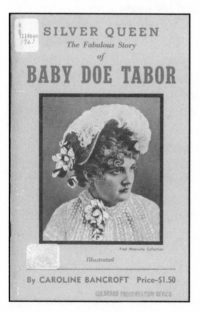

The 1950 booklet Silver Queen *cemented Bancroft's reputation as an able writer of vivid Colorado histories. Bancroft followed it with* Augusta Tabor; Her Side of the Scandal *in 1955, in which an "anguished Augusta" recounts losing her husband to Baby Doe. (Colorado Historical Society)*

about pioneers who overcame the severe hardships of a challenging frontier. Readers wanted romance, and Caroline gave them what they wanted.

Once, when friend and colleague David Halaas "called her" on altering facts, Bancroft replied: "Go ahead. Do anything you want. I'm the grande dame of Colorado history." Bancroft's proprietary claim as Colorado history's grande dame has merit if genealogy proves ownership. She attributed her interest in the state's past to her paternal grandfather, Frederick J. Bancroft, MD, who cofounded the State Historical and Natural History Society of Colorado (later renamed the Colorado Historical Society) in 1879 and served as its first president for seventeen years. Nicknamed "the jovial giant" by patients and friends, the six-foot, four-inch, 300-pound Denver surgeon was often seen making housecalls driving his horse and buggy with springs twice as strong on his side as on the other. Dr. Bancroft served four years in the Civil War and for a time was post surgeon at Fort Monroe, Virginia. There he offered his medical services to a distinguished war prisoner who was brought to the fort: Jefferson Davis, the ailing president of the defeated Confederacy. According to Edmond J. A. Rogers, MD, who eulogized the surgeon in the *Denver Medical Times* of 1903, Davis refused the Yankee's courtesy.

At age thirty-two, Bancroft came by the Overland Stage in 1866 to Denver, an outpost between the 100th meridian and the Rocky Mountains. The raw, high prairie town had begun to look green wherever the 1,000 miles of the new, lateral City Ditch flowed. Caroline insisted that her grandfather brought dandelions from his native Connecticut to brighten the drab Denver landscape.

The doctor made a fortune in Colorado from his medical practice, agriculture, and buying square miles of mountain and plain with senior water rights. He quickly became a leader in Denver's medical, banking, and educational institutions. While many contended that the only good Indian was a dead one, Ute Chief Colorow was Bancroft's friend. The two men often swapped horse stories as they sat on the front porch of Bancroft's medical office, wrote *Denver Post* newsman Bill Hosokawa in 1984.

Caroline's paternal grandmother, Mary Caroline Jarvis, had traveled by stagecoach and railroad from Brooklyn, New York, to Colorado Territory in 1870, seeking a cure for her tuberculosis. She

Caroline's grandfather, Frederick J. Bancroft, MD, and family are photographed at their first home on the southwest corner of what is today the Sixteenth Street Mall at Stout Street. (Western History Department, Denver Public Library)

joined thousands of TB sufferers—the "one-lunged army," healthy Denverites called them—who came for the town's high and dry climate hoping to regain their health. According to Caroline, her grandmother stepped off the train at Union Station and fell hemorrhaging into the arms of the Denver Pacific Railroad's chief surgeon, bachelor Frederick J. Bancroft. Mary Caroline lived with Episcopal bishop and Mrs. George M. Randall until her marriage a year later to Bancroft. The bride's millionaire father gave the couple their first home, described by Jerome C. Smiley's 1901 *History of Denver* as a "handsome, one-story brick residence" on the southwest corner of what is today the Sixteenth Street Mall at Stout Street. Later, Bancroft built an office block at that location. The couple's three children were born in their first home: Mary McLean in 1871; George Jarvis, Caroline's father, in 1873; and Frederick Wolcott in 1880.

By 1880, Denver's population had soared to nearly 36,000. Thermal inversion in winter blanketed the city. Coal powered everything that electricity does today, and coal smoke fouled the air. Open irrigation ditches carried polluted water. Soil was saddened from cesspools and privies. "Good" neighborhoods were those farthest away from increasing commercial growth and minority populations. Today's Lower Downtown had been the original neighborhood of the elite, but newer and higher land became fashionable. The Bancroft family joined the exodus of cattle barons and mining kings to Capitol Hill. Their red brick, gabled Victorian home with two-story bowed windows at 1775 Grant Street, "The Avenue of Kings," had an uninterrupted view of mountains to the west and prairie to the east.

The 1880s were also a time when religious institutions followed their congregations eastward, building increasingly grand structures in the vicinity of Grant Street, an area dense with extravagant mansions and places of worship. Denverites hired architects to design brick and stone structures that imitated their remembered but distant homes. The Immaculate Conception Cathedral Association had bought eight lots at East Colfax Avenue and Logan Street for a French Gothic building to serve Denver's burgeoning Roman Catholic population. The Central Presbyterian Church, formerly at Eighteenth and Champa Streets, now filled the entire corner lot at 1660 Sherman Street. Temple Emanuel would move to its new, Moorish-style synagogue in 1898 at East Sixteenth Avenue and Pearl Street to house Colorado's largest Jewish congregation. Meanwhile, St. John's Episcopal Cathedral in the Wilderness had moved uptown by 1881 to Twentieth and Welton Streets. ("Wilderness" refers to the Denver cathedral's beginnings when the nearest Episcopal church was 700 miles away in Kansas.)[2]

The second-generation Bancrofts attended local private schools. George went to the Episcopalian Jarvis Hall, a high school endowed by his maternal grandparents in the new suburb of Montclair. Later he graduated as a mining engineer in Stanford University's first graduation class of 1895; a classmate was future US president Herbert Hoover. George's choice of an unremarkable West Coast college departed from the Denver norm. His peers preferred the Ivy Leagues.

After graduation, George returned to Denver, where he met and fell in love with Ethel Norton. She had come from Troy, New York, with her mother and brother Ray, who was desperately ill from tuberculosis. Ray died within a year of the move west. Ethel's finishing school education and membership in the Society of Colonial Dames in the State of New York impressed class-conscious Denverites with their admiration for eastern respectability.

Ethel, twenty-one, and George were married in what society-page editors called the 1899 social event of the season. One hundred fifty of the "Smart Set" and Denver's Old Guard families walked up the

Caroline and her father, George Jarvis Bancroft, photographed in 1901. (Western History Department, Denver Public Library)

hill from St. John's Cathedral to the wedding reception at the Bancroft mansion. Pioneers who now are place-names—Bishop J. F. Spalding, Moses Hallett, David Moffat—celebrated one of the last gatherings of civic leaders who had been present at Denver's beginnings. Mary Caroline Bancroft, age fifty-nine, died shortly after the wedding, and Dr. Bancroft died four years later.

Immediately after their wedding, the couple moved to Cripple Creek, where George worked as an advisor to the gold-mining interests of family friends. Western mining at the turn of the century was particularly depressed after the 1893 Silver Crash, but its boom-and-bust nature appealed to the gambler instinct in George. He traveled the West and Mexico for years, finding work and investing good money in bad mines. His financial affairs were often desperate, though he had inherited a sizable fortune.

By 1902, George and Ethel had moved to a red brick Victorian house at 1081 Downing Street on Denver's Capitol Hill, where Ethel spent the rest of her life. "Such a quiet place in the country," Caroline said, remembering the vacant lots and unpaved roads of east Denver. George struggled to pay the $5,200 mortgage. Ethel, a woman with frugality in her bones, raised their two daughters, Caroline, born in

Ethel Norton Bancroft, pictured in 1909 with Peggy, age 4, and Caroline, age 9, raised her daughters to be fashionable members of society despite the family's erratic income. (Western History Department,Denver Public Library)

1900, and Peggy, born in 1905. George traveled throughout the girls' childhood, searching for ore strikes and sending money home when he could. Out of necessity, Ethel eventually rented out the second floor of their home. "Father was up and down financially," Caroline said of her early years.[3]

George Bancroft evidently lacked the pioneer spirit of his parents. Still, his revolutionary concept of diverting Western Slope water to high and dry Denver guaranteed an adequate water supply for years to come. In 1899, railroad builder David Moffat hired young George to survey the terrain across the Continental Divide's rugged crest and to advise on the exact location of a tunnel bore for railroad track. George mapped the tunnel site. More significantly, he convinced Moffat that the tunnel could carry both track and water pipe. Moffat and Bancroft individually bought water claims covering the area where the project was to be located.

Moffat's dream to build the railroad bankrupted him, but the Moffat Tunnel was later built as two tunnels, one for track and one for water. Moffat and Bancroft sold their water claims to the Denver Water Commission, a critical purchase for a city that averages sixteen inches of annual precipitation.[4]

The self-proclaimed social arbiter of Denver's "Sacred 36," Mrs. Crawford Hill, in 1908 dictated a social register for the city of Denver. The George Bancroft family was among the anointed. "I've never not been in the *Blue Book*," Caroline proudly said. Although she decreed in the 1970s that "there is no 'society' in Denver any more," she cherished being in the book decades after its first publication.[5] Longtime friend James R. Hartley understood that Caroline's dominating, outspoken personality, which outraged many contemporaries, also camouflaged a sense of insecurity. "She was a woman alone. The *Blue Book* was Denver's only notable listing of distinction," one that affirmed her importance. Inclusion in the book didn't require wealth, although the perception was that it did. Caroline's frugality, like her mother's, meant operating on a rigid budget, recycling clothing and furniture until they wore out, and making do or doing without. "You were lucky to get a peanut at her cocktail parties," recalls Hartley.

The stalwart Ethel raised Caroline and Peggy as young ladies, putting the best face on a negative cash flow. The sisters wore hats and white gloves on Sundays at St. John's, sitting with their mother in the Bancroft pew behind Mrs. Hill's. They were taught to defer to adults. The girls took ballroom dancing lessons and learned to ride horseback. The Bancrofts kept their horses at the Wentworth Stables at 1120 Corona Street. "We would get on our horses and ride to Cheesman Park," Bancroft said, "and from then on it was open prairie."[6]

Although *Blue Book* families sent their daughters to private schools, household economics required that Caroline and Peggy attend public schools. "If my father had any money when I was growing up, his family saw very little of it," she told Melrose in 1977. "I went to the new North High School, which was the 'in' school at the time. My parents thought there were too many ladies-of-the-evening hanging around the first East High School" on the square block at Ninetieth and Stout Streets. By then George, whom she described in 1972 to *Denver Post* reporter Olga Curtis as an "alcoholic bastard," had gam-

bled away his inheritance—"half a million dollars on mining specula-
tion, whiskey, and women."

The two daughters were a study in contrasts. Caroline was dark-
haired, large-framed, opinionated, and independent. She ran away
from home at age seventeen. "I saved up my money, escaped to New
York and got a job as a showgirl understudy in the Ziegfeld Night
Follies. Only I never appeared on stage. My mother was horrified and
sent a batch of relatives after me," she told Bill Hosakawa in 1984.
Sister Peggy, however, succeeded. The blond, blue-eyed, petite
beauty quit high school to escape her parents' constant arguing and,
following her older sister's example, also fled to Manhattan. Peggy
became a showgirl in nightclubs and the Ziegfeld Follies, later marrying the wealthy Robert LeBaron of Washington, D.C. She returned
to Denver only when family funerals demanded it.

From girlhood, Caroline's attitude toward men was shaped by her
father. To the Historical Society's David Halaas, she identified the
defining moment of her relationship with men by recalling a time
when she was riding horseback with her father. They had crossed a
mountain stream infested with thickets, and George's horse was
stuck. He beat and whipped the horse. Caroline said, "His hand came
down and down. I screamed at him, 'Don't! Don't!' He continued
to whip the horse and I kept screaming. At that moment I decided
never again would I trust a man."

George and Ethel divorced in 1923 after a court battle that was
enthusiastically reported in Denver newspapers. In a culture that
scorned divorce, Ethel became the target of gossip after court testimony exposed George's philandering and failure to provide ade-
quately for his family. The rumors grew uglier when George filed a
lawsuit against Ethel, charging her with "unmotherly, cold-blooded
mercenary" acceptance of money from "a certain man living in Troy,
New York," which led to the father's "sorrow, grief, worry, and
humiliation."[7] The lawsuit was dismissed: Ethel's cousins in Troy
paid for Caroline's education at Smith College in Massachusetts
because Ethel could not. George died, nearly bankrupt, in 1945.

With just a finishing school education, Ethel at age forty-seven
began working for the Denver Public Schools, a radical move for a
woman of her age and social status. Then she enrolled at the Univer-

sity of Denver, earning both bachelor's and master's degrees by 1934. She retired at age sixty-eight as a DPS social worker. Caroline dedicated her 1958 *Gulch of Gold: A History of Central City,* to her mother, "one daughter's fortress." Informed of her cancer at age eighty-one, Ethel "did her spring housecleaning, handwashed the window curtains, distributed her personal jewelry, and made a list of the seating of mourners who would attend her funeral," wrote Caroline's great friend, Mary Coyle Chase, in the *Rocky Mountain News.* Then Ethel went to St. Luke's Hospital, where she died in 1959.

Caroline graduated from Smith College in 1923 and stayed on the East Coast, since "my idea of Denver was that it was in the sticks."[8] She taught in an elementary school in Connecticut because she needed a steady income, and she liked the position's summer option to chaperone student tours on the Holland American Line in return for free passage. She took advantage of the opportunity. "Once we landed, I was on my own. I tried to go somewhere different every summer." Caroline roamed Europe, going as far as the Holy Land, Egypt, India, and Tibet. Traveling alone when most women of her era did not venture far from the hearth, Caroline was clearly "liberated" long before her gender owned that term. "I've been liberated all my life," she told newspaper reporter Rebecca Norris of the Granby, Colorado, *Sky-Hi News* in 1982. "Anybody who's got the guts and brains can be liberated."

Frances Melrose's article underscores Caroline's independence: "I've done so many things. People ask why I never married, because I've had several fiancés. But I always thought of a trip or book I had to write when it came to setting a wedding date. While my Park Avenue friends were changing diapers, I was riding a camel in Egypt."

Caroline taught for four years and then quit to do research for popular magazines and do freelance writing. Her essays appeared as an occasional column in the *Denver Post* and the *New York Post.* On a travel assignment to Europe in 1929, Caroline interviewed John Galsworthy in London, George Bernard Shaw in Ireland, and Hendrik Van Loon in Holland for the *Evening Post.*[9] She spent six months in Paris when it was the center for talented expatriate Americans. She called that time "my glamour period," wrote Curtis: "I had a lot of brass and a few connections, and I was a celebrity chaser. I had visions

An avid world traveler, Bancroft visited Egypt in 1927. (Colorado Historical Society)

of myself writing the great American novel, living all over the world and marrying a millionaire. At the last minute, I was always afraid I'd wind up with a husband like my father."

In 1928, before her "glamour period" began, she needed a steady writing job. At Caroline's request, her "patron," Mrs. Crawford Hill, recommended the aspiring writer to the wily and infamous copublisher of the *Denver Post*, Frederick G. Bonfils. According to Caroline, Bonfils owed Mrs. Hill a favor after the doyenne of Denver society successfully steered his membership application to the Denver Country Club around the protests of indignant club members. (Interestingly, club records show that Bonfils was never a member.) Caroline was confident of being hired. "I sailed into F.G.'s office and announced that it was time he had a book editor on his staff, a position that might improve the paper's image." At a time when many looked down their noses at the newspaper, which Caroline described as a "libelous, sensation-seeking rag," she said she knew Denverites who had it delivered secretly to their servants' entrances.[10]

"When my friends heard I was working for the *Post*, they thought I might as well have joined a house of joy. Newspaper people, while they are much in demand now, weren't considered socially acceptable in that day, any more than actors were," Caroline recalled.[11] The *Post* offered her more than a $25 weekly salary and a byline. She didn't just want a newspaper job, she also wanted to be part of Denver's social scene. By promoting her column through *Blue Book* audiences like the Monday Literary Club, the Tuesday Book Club, and the Junior League, Caroline could maintain her high society connections with Old Guard friends such as Mrs. George Berger of 124 Layfayette Street and Mrs. William W. Grant, who lived in the Richthofen Castle in the Montclair neighborhood.

The *Post*'s managing editor, William C. Shepherd, would frequently "forget" to sign her paychecks, and Caroline would panic. He didn't read her columns because "a book page was the last thing he was interested in. 'Shep' read sports, sex, and society columns," said Caroline. Each time she wasn't paid, she complained to Bonfils, who would order Shep to sign the check. The paycheck crisis became a seminal moment in her career when Bonfils suggested a way to get Shep as a reader. Bonfils pointed out that Caroline had entree to prominent old-timers that ordinary *Post* reporters didn't have. Bonfils told her to interview and then write stories about Colorado's aging generation of first settlers. His strategy worked; from then on she was paid promptly. The old-timer stories were Caroline's first venture in writing about Colorado history.

After Bonfils died in 1933, Caroline quit the newspaper, leaving with an appreciation of Colorado history and a goal to write its stories. To learn more about her state she enrolled in the graduate school at the University of Denver, nicknamed "Tramway Tech" for the many DU students who rode to school in the overhead electric trolleys of the city's transportation system. By 1943 she had earned a master's degree in western history.[12] Her thesis on Central City became the source for *Gulch of Gold*, published in 1959. The 354-page book established the format for her booklets: an all-knowing narrator, undocumented dialogue, characters the author felt were "consistent" with her original research, hand-drawn maps, vintage photographs, and a vivid picture of the way things could have been.

Gulch of Gold was the first book to detail Central City's evolution from mining town to mountain resort.

Gulch of Gold points out that Central City was dubbed "the richest square mile on earth" after the 1859 discovery of the first lode gold in gulches around the mining town, elevation 8,500 feet. The bonanza gave real meaning to the "Pikes Peak or Bust" gold rush. Gold fever swelled the town's population to nearly 20,000 in the 1870s, but by 1925, mining had trickled down to nothing. Central City's population shrank to 400, and the glorious opera house, built in 1871, became an abandoned wreck.

The University of Denver was given title to the opera house by the heirs of Gilpin County pioneer Peter McFarlane. DU's theater department saw a priceless opportunity to present significant productions to Coloradans. Soon the Central City Opera House Association was formed to succeed the university's ownership. Despite a global depression and Central City's isolation by narrow, frightening dirt roads on steep grades, the CCOHA ignored all naysayers. The concept became a crusade, and a summer drama and music festival became a reality in 1932 when the opera house reopened. The event starred the wildly popular actress Lillian Gish in the title role of *Camille*. Denver society, dressed in Victorian-period costumes, and the national media turned out for opening night. NBC Radio broadcast the festivities.[13]

Central City became the destination of every Brahmin in Denver, and to be on a CCOHA committee meant automatic membership in Denver society. Caroline, a charter member of the association, worked with scores of volunteers to clean the opera house. At the request of "Aunt" Anne Evans, as Caroline called the daughter of former territorial governor John Evans, who had founded DU, she also served on the festival's publicity committee. Caroline researched the town's history, read its vintage newspapers, interviewed residents who stubbornly refused to leave, and rescued mining artifacts and old photographs from indifferent owners. She used the material for *Gulch of Gold* and also for her first booklet, which she self-published in 1946, *A Guide to Central City*. "I spent $500 of my own money to print 5,000 copies and sold them all for 50 cents each," she told Curtis. Caroline had found her own mother lode: popular history. Writing it became her career.

Also in 1946, Caroline purchased for $125 the only home she ever bought, a miner's house on Casto Hill down the gulch from the opera house. Her Central City friend of forty years, Kay Russell, remembers how her husband Bill and Caroline "used to argue into the wee hours on the many occasions she came to visit, and the next day continuing without either budging an inch. Then she and I would jeep into her beloved high country to the music of mountains and gin and tonic at various 'libation stations,' a phrase she coined and which is now famous." Another devoted friend, the glamorous Mrs. Emma Wilson, proprietor of Central City's Glory Hole Bar, hosted a large party for Caroline after the first edition of *A Guide to Central City* sold out. At the celebration, "Emmy" gave Caroline a tin necklace made of Central City keyholes along with a rhyme that suggested the objects had been invaluable peepholes to the Central City chronicler[14] (Bancroft Files). For picnics, opening nights at the opera, or Glory Hole parties, Caroline sipped from a sterling silver straw she never left home without.

Gradually, Caroline parlayed her 1946 success into a full-time career by researching, writing, and self-publishing her local histories. She filled mail orders from the Downing Street home, and with her mother drove the state's tourist circuit to restock hotel, drugstore, and curio store shelves with Bancroft publications. Because Caroline revised and reissued several booklets under different titles, the total number published is unknown. For example, *A Guide to Central City* became *Historic Central City* in 1951. Caroline split *Trail Ridge Country, Estes Park and Grand Lake* into two booklets so that tourists in Estes Park didn't have to read about Grand Lake and vice versa. Alan Swallow, a DU English professor and owner of the Swallow Press, published the hardcover *Colorful Colorado* in 1958, while Caroline published the same text in paperback form minus the bibliography and index.

If Denver-on-the-Platte had a café society, Caroline was part of it from the 1930s on. Her "chums" or "pals," as she called them, included Alan Swallow, Mary Coyle Chase, Colorado's first Pulitzer Prize winner for the play *Harvey*; and watercolor artist and newspaper photographer Herndon Davis, who painted *The Face on the Barroom Floor* in Central City's Teller House Bar during a party late one night in 1936. Prominent local artist Vance Kirkland and muralist Allen True, who painted the murals inside the State Capitol dome, were lively café society members. So were national writers of the West like Lucius Beebe, Marshall Sprague, and Mari Sandoz, who joined the others when they were in town. Flamboyantly beautiful Denverite Eleanor Weckbaugh and Evalyn Walsh MacLean, owner of the forty-four-carat Hope diamond, were society regulars as well.

For decades Caroline was one of the most photographed women in Denver. No social, civic, or literary function seemed complete without her name on the roster. Her name was news in society columns, and although she couldn't afford membership in the Denver Country Club, she was so regularly photographed there that many assumed she belonged. When the post–World War II influx of wealthy newcomers to Denver gained access to the city's exclusive private clubs, Caroline deplored the changing of the guard. She savored inside gossip about a new-money hopeful who offered $50,000 to the *Blue Book* editor to be included in the social register.[15]

While Caroline lectured to the public about Colorado history, she lectured privately about issues of social importance. She eliminated a quarter of the city's population through her edict that "nobody who was anybody" lived north of East Colfax. In her day, young men went to Ivy League schools and women to their sister colleges. If you hadn't inherited furniture, you bought it at one downtown store, Davis & Shaw. Nobody who was anybody ever called it the "Denver Country Club," because it was "patently obvious" that The Country Club, established in 1887, was the only one that mattered. "The others are for parvenus," which she dismissed, "the others" being Cherry Hills Country Club and Green Gables Country Club.

The Centennial State's history, however, was her number 1 priority. "Caroline probably knew more about Colorado than anyone of her time: its history, geography, people, mining camps, jeep trails," says David Halaas. And as the "self-appointed sentinel of Colorado history," she was vigilant in correcting the errors of others. Once, while addressing the Historical Society, Governor Richard Lamm pronounced the state's name "Col-o-RAD-oh" rather than "Col-o-RAHD-oh," the pronunciation Caroline preferred. The next morning she telephoned the governor to scold him; Lamm apologized and wrote her a letter promising "to do better."[16]

Melrose remembers that Caroline sent stinging rebukes to *Rocky Mountain News* reporters who mixed up the facts. "In the City Room, we had this philosophy that if you didn't get a postcard from Caroline, you weren't working." Virginia Rockwell, society reporter for the *Denver Post* in 1946, recalls that Caroline "trudged up the stairs at the Champa Street newspaper building and gave me hell for what I'd written the day before." Sandra Dallas knew Caroline as "a vibrant, opinionated woman, who, when stirred, showed the wrath of an angry god. She vilified anybody who made errors," including Pulitzer Prize–winning novelist James Michener in his 1976 *Centennial,* a historical novel of Colorado.

An even worse sin was failing to agree with her. "She often wrote in book reviews that if the author had just read her writing on the sub-

> ## Empire welcomes correspondence
>
> ## Battling historians
>
> Olga Curtis' most unusual article, *The battling historians* (Jan. 16), was read with a great deal of gusto and pleasure. We received countless telephone calls from delighted friends.
>
> I am puzzled by the one statement that appears on page 14. It seems as though Caroline (Bancroft) was in the habit of "racing camels over the Arabian Desert." Who won the race, Caroline or the camel?
>
> Thanks again for a very objective and revealing article.
>
> Fred and Jo Mazzulla
> Denver
>
> © Colorado Historical Society

In 1972, Empire Magazine *profiled the "battling historians": Fred Mazzulla and Caroline Bancroft. Once good friends, the two developed an animosity that lasted the rest of their lives. Mazzulla got the last word with this sardonic letter to the editor.* (Empire Magazine, Denver Post)

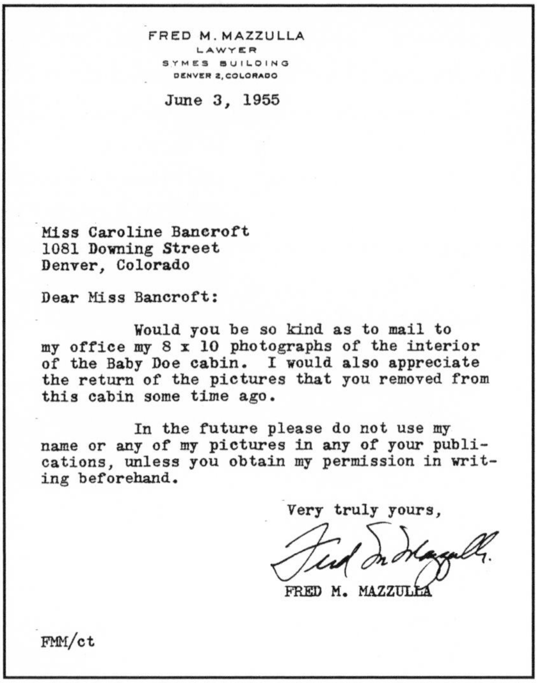

FRED M. MAZZULLA
LAWYER
SYMES BUILDING
DENVER 2, COLORADO

June 3, 1955

Miss Caroline Bancroft
1081 Downing Street
Denver, Colorado

Dear Miss Bancroft:

Would you be so kind as to mail to
my office my 8 x 10 photographs of the interior
of the Baby Doe cabin. I would also appreciate
the return of the pictures that you removed from
this cabin some time ago.

In the future please do not use my
name or any of my pictures in any of your publications, unless you obtain my permission in writing beforehand.

Very truly yours,

FRED M. MAZZULLA

FMM/ct

A letter from Fred Mazzulla to Caroline, showing the obvious disdain that had developed between the once good friends. (Western History Department, Denver Public Library)

ject, he or she wouldn't have made such a foolish mistake. But when the author did as Caroline suggested, Caroline might charge plagiarism," Dallas wrote in the most balanced of all of Caroline's obituaries.

Caroline's caustic tongue made many enemies, and she relished the feuds. The most famous was with Denver photo-historian Fred Mazzulla, her former "pal." Fred and his wife, Jo, had been friends of long standing. The three often traveled the state together researching historical sites, and Fred helped Caroline illustrate her booklets by lending her vintage photographs from his collection of 250,000.[17] After Caroline spread the rumor that he had made a pass at her, the Mazzullas were furious. The three never reconciled. "She steals my stuff to write a unique brand of history, a series of misquotes held together with stolen passages and pictures," Mazzulla told Olga Curtis in a *Post* feature story, "The Battling Historians."[18] Caroline responded in kind, saying of Mazzulla that "as a historian, Fred's a

118

remarkable collector. Some of his books had to be ghostwritten. He misrepresents his pictures. He's just not reliable." She added, however: "I improve history when it seems logical. My characters talk, dress up and get involved in things because history has to have popular appeal. I put in the truth and the folklore, too."

Regarding her invented dialogue, Caroline cut herself a little slack in her 1974 interview in *Where* magazine: "I cannot defend the exact dialogue in my books. I don't know that that person said that thing at that moment. But they jolly well better had because I had done so much research that I knew it was the kind of thing they would have said. I did what's known as popular history or fictionalized history, except it's almost no fiction." Denver book reviewer Mollie Lee Beresford once objected to Caroline's dialogue inventions. Caroline responded, "Well, Mollie Lee, no one will ever know but you. The rest are all dead."[19]

In the *Where* interview, Caroline identified her audience as "intelligent tourists" who, before her booklets were published, "didn't have anything to read. I wanted to write something that would be easy to read, would be true, would be absolutely documented. I wanted to write something that would be light on the pocketbook, light in the suitcase and also authentic—solid in terms of research. What looks like fiction is something I've historically researched."

Those who support Caroline's paradoxical stand—that she wrote fictionalized history that was "almost no fiction"—point to the fact that an astounding number of her booklets have sold, that six are still in print, and that tourists and residents have learned much from the author about Colorado and its past. A prominent defender was Liston E. Leyendecker, a professor of American history at Colorado State University, who urged critics to judge Caroline's booklets "by the conventions of her era, not ours. If she can get folks interested in Colorado history, then they can go to a university, and we can teach them from there."[20] Another Coloradan with a broad knowledge of the state's past is Callae Buell Gilman, who observed that "Caroline didn't hurt things much."

Her most eloquent defender, David Halaas, cites three contributions Caroline made: she interested people in the Tabor stories and in Colorado—as James Michener did in his novel *Centennial*, "a terrible book but still more real than texts"; she influenced two generations

You won't find Caroline's booklets in Fred's library, or his in hers, but they didn't mind show-ing off their own. Fred uses those stacks for research. Caroline is displaying her booklets. (Empire Magazine, Denver Post)

of local historians; and, as a writer, she was "an awesome figure, as impressive as all hell." Halaas adds: "If we didn't have Caroline Ban-croft or Mari Sandoz, we'd have to invent them. Mari Sandoz and Caroline were friends and kindred spirits. Sandoz's *Crazy Horse*, a brilliant book, captures the times and essence of Chief Crazy Horse better than anyone else. Likewise, Michael Shaara's historical novel about the Civil War, *Killer Angels*, touches us. Great writers touch us and capture our hearts. There are some things you cannot do in an academic book."

Audiences continue to be touched by Caroline's love story of Baby Doe and Horace Tabor, one that reflects the drama and spirit of a reckless, opulent era. In Tabor's dramatic deathbed scene, Caroline's version has Tabor uttering his last words to the sobbing Baby Doe: "Hang on to the Matchless. It will make millions again." These words resonate in dozens of later Baby Doe publications. For exam-ple, one of the most poignant moments in *The Ballad of Baby Doe*, an opera by Douglas Moore and John LaTouche that premiered in Central City in 1956, has Baby Doe promising her husband that she will always hold on to the Matchless Mine.

One afternoon in 1982, Halaas and a Historical Society colleague discussed with Caroline the booklet and Tabor's dying command, "Hang on to the Matchless." Halaas commented on the beauty of the five famous words. "Well," Caroline said, "I made them up." It was a remarkable admission of invented dialogue that is now legend.

The fued and potential lawsuit that Caroline threatened over the Moore/LaTouche opera is definitely not legend. She created an uproar, insisting that her years-long study of the Baby Doe tragedy gave her sole ownership of the story. Caroline hired a lawyer to defend her rights. Frank Ricketson, Jr., president of the CCOHA, in 1954 complained to Donald Oenslager, the internationally recognized stage designer for the new opera, that Caroline "seems to have arrogated unto herself the exclusive right to all of Colorado's early history, that Baby Doe is her own personal character and property." Oenslager suggested Ricketson pay Bancroft $250 and name her historical advisor "to keep her quiet." Caroline accepted the offer and the opera debuted in 1956.[21]

The Tabor research became the most important research in Caroline's life. Because of it, Melrose wrote in 1977, the Leadville Assembly restored the Matchless Mine shack. "I personally raised the funds for that museum by soliciting little donations of $5, $10, and $15," Caroline said. A feud erupted over a date for the museum's opening day, with the town council in opposition to Caroline. "I really don't start these things," she protested to Melrose. "It's usually someone who has a vendetta against me, for some reason. Personally, I can't hold a grudge for five minutes."

Melrose describes another event that came out of the Baby Doe story: Caroline's "collaboration on a tombstone for Baby Doe's daughter, Silver Dollar, 32 years after she was scalded to death in a Chicago rooming house." Melrose quotes Caroline: "Her mother always maintained that Silver Dollar was in a convent and would not admit that the woman who died was her daughter." Bancroft, Chicago newspaperman Tom Peavy, and Bert Baker, a Minneapolis resident, paid for the stone in Chicago's Holy Sepulchre Cemetery.

Bancroft, in period garb, attends the July 1953 dedication of the Matchless Mine whose preservation she championed. Crowded in the shaft house, the celebrants include (from left) Fred Mazzulla (kneeling with camera), socialite Eleanor Weckbaugh, Edith Neale Easton, and Bancroft. (Western History Department, Denver Public Library)

Caroline's second most popular booklet is *The Unsinkable Mrs. Brown*. It was published in 1956, decades before descendants of Margaret and J.J. Brown released critical family papers to document the facts of Mrs. Brown's extraordinary life. Readers enjoyed Caroline's story about the spunky westerner who saved a boatload of people from drowning in 1912 by rowing a lifeboat away from the sinking *Titanic*. As Maggie ("Molly" was a Hollywood invention) rowed, she sang lustily to quiet hysterical passengers. Her courage won the world's admiration and, finally, Denver's. When Mrs. Brown returned to America after the disaster, she told reporters she'd had "typical Brown luck. I'm unsinkable." Molly Brown became a legend in her own time, and reigns as one of Colorado's most colorful characters. Gene Fowler, a *Post* reporter whose rakehell journalistic style typified writing of the 1930s, wrote the first and fictitious chapter about her in his 1933 book, *Timber Line*. He turned Molly Brown's *Titanic* episode and social climbing struggles into a hilarious story. *Reader's*

Digest ran the chapter as fact. Fowler sold the movie rights of the entire book to Metro-Goldwyn-Mayer, and a 1960 Broadway musical became the 1963 MGM film, *The Unsinkable Molly Brown*, starring Debbie Reynolds and Harve Presnell. Brown's legend continued in the 1997 film, *Titanic*, with Kathy Bates in the Unsinkable role.

Caroline began her research on Molly Brown in 1935. Once again, as she complains in her introduction to *The Unsinkable Mrs. Brown*: "Many difficulties developed. Although I knew of Fowler's propensity to exaggerate and had not expected to find truth in his telling, I did expect quantities of old newspaper stories about Mrs. Brown to check out. Many did not. Documented records were scarce and other reliable sources proved almost impossible to find." Compounding the research crisis, she says, "The most formidable difficulty was the attitude of her son Lawrence, a Leadville resident, who alternated between a desire to see his mother immortalized and panic that a serious writer would expose the truth." Caroline shelved the project. In 1949, Larry Brown died. His sister, Helen Benziger, according to Caroline, "had made a fine marriage in the East, had put her Western past completely away, had no interest in Colorado, and had dropped all of her Denver friends. ... She preferred to have everything about her mother forgotten. Helen wanted neither the myth nor the truth perpetuated."

Caroline returned to the topic in 1955 and shortly before her forty-four-page booklet was published the next year, Walter Lord's book about the *Titanic* disaster, *A Night to Remember*, became a best-seller. Caroline says, "In essence my view varied hardly at all from his. But his was more detailed, and I elaborated my version with some of his thorough research before the booklet appeared."

The booklet begins with a typically enticing Bancroft lead: "Margaret Tobin of Hannibal, Missouri, was a high-spirited, bosomy Irish girl whose wavy auburn hair crowned a head alive with ambition. She was the daughter of a ditchdigger for the gas works. But, as Maggie looked about her at the thriving, noisy rail-and-riverboat center, she dreamed of greater things than the life of a laborer's daughter."

Caroline follows Maggie's path to Leadville, where she marries James J. Brown. The booklet details J.J.'s spectacular success as superintendent of the Little Jonny gold mine; the birth of their two children; their move to Denver, where Maggie is snubbed by its

123

On location, Telluride, Colorado. M. G. M. photo,
September, 1963. "The Unsinkable Molly Brown"

To Wish You
A Happy New Year--

Caroline Bancroft and Harve Presnell at Telluride, Colorado, on location for the filming of the 1963 MGM movie, "The Unsinkable Molly Brown," starring Debbie Reynolds and Presnell. (Western History Department, Denver Public Library) exclusive high society; her travels abroad; the *Titanic* episode; her friendships with Newport, Rhode Island, multimillionaires; and finally her death in 1932 at the Barbizon Club Hotel in New York City. Like the other Bancroft Booklets, *The Unsinkable Mrs. Brown* uses the inside back cover to credit institutions and individuals for research aid, photographs, criticism, and proofreading. No source takes specific responsibility for facts in the text.

Caroline's "pal" Lucius Beebe reviewed the booklet in his Nevada newspaper, *The Territorial Enterprise and Virginia City News.* He described the running commentary as "couched in a sort of pidgin English" that portrayed Margaret Brown as a woman who "wanted in where nobody wanted her, least of all Denver's established 'society' which itself had only arrived the week previous and presented a hideous spectacle of provincial snobbism." Beebe praises the Bancroft Booklets as "reasonably factual," adding that they offered tourists "suggestions of Colorado's spacious and wonderful past before it fell victim to the delusions of progress inherent in overpopulation and a gradual disappearance of the highly individualistic men and women who started it all."

A more severe critic of Caroline's popular booklet was Margaret Brown's great-grand-daughter, Muffet Laurie Brown. When she began to research her family's history, she learned that "apparently Caroline Bancroft had the nerve to send our family an autographed copy of her insulting biography."[22]

Kristen Iversen's 1999 biography, *Molly Brown: Unraveling the Myth,* uses the Brown letters, journals, court records, newspaper articles, and family memoirs unavailable to Caroline forty-three years earlier. Iversen writes:

> The "character" of the mythical Molly Brown represents what we want to believe about the West just as the real West is disappearing. The western frontier embodied America's desire to believe in a "pure" western character, strong, independent, unfettered by culture.
>
> The facts don't support the myths. As folklore, the legend of Molly Brown rivals the stories of Calamity Jane, Billy the Kid, and even Paul Bunyan. The first writers, Gene Fowler and Caroline Bancroft, strongly influenced by the colorful, inflammatory tabloid style

of journalism in the late 1930s, found few facts to feed their stories. So they invented, and a legend was born.

Armed with voluminous and virgin data, Iversen reveals Margaret Brown as a woman different from all earlier portrayals. As an adult, Brown studied at the Carnegie Institute in New York City. Her letters from abroad reveal an astute observer, fluent in several languages. The Brown family was listed in Denver's social record from the year they moved to Denver from Leadville. While Caroline meanly told *Reader's Digest* editors that Brown bought her French Legion of Honor medal "in a hockshop," Iversen documents that Brown received France's highest honor in 1932 for recognition of her work in France during World War I. Iversen's book is the first full-length biography of a woman who crusaded for the rights of children and miners and for women's suffrage. The author conjectures that because Brown had led a relatively independent life, she was "cast as aggressive, flamboyant and unnatural" by those people, usually men, who were threatened with the notion of social change.

Writing, publishing, and marketing her work exhausted Bancroft, who led an equally exhaustive social life. Despite a robust appearance, she battled both tuberculosis and cancer several times. In 1967 she turned over her cottage industry to Johnson Books, a decision that enabled her to continue receiving royalties while tapering off her writing activities. Caroline stopped writing booklets in 1969, and in 1975 sold the Bancroft home, moving to the nearby Waldman Apartments in the Cheesman Park neighborhood, where she spent her last ten years. She died in her sleep at age eighty-five and was buried in the family plot at Fairmount Cemetery.

J. Robert Welch, Caroline's trustee and personal representative of her estate, estimated in 2002 that a million Bancroft Booklets had been sold. Caroline's will directed that the trust income from investments and booklet royalties be paid to the Western History Department at the Denver Public Library and to the Colorado Historical Society. Distributions in excess of $500,000 have been made to the two insti-

Caroline's "favorite" portrait was painted in 1924 in Paris by John Trumbee. (Western History Department, Denver Public Library)

tutions, an impressive gift from a woman who loved Colorado more than her creature comforts.

The library's Western History/Genealogy department divides its annual Bancroft income into four parts as stipulated in Caroline's will. Eighty percent goes to capital improvements and equipment; acquisition of maps, books, and manuscripts; and indexing, processing, and cataloging of manuscripts. The fourth part, 20 percent, funds the Caroline Bancroft History Prize, which annually "recognizes an author who has opened our eyes and brought new perspectives about the West, through excellent writing, original style and thorough research." Recipients include Robert G. Athearn (1987), Elliot West (1990 and 1999), Stephen J. Leonard (1994), and Patricia Trenton (1996).

The Colorado Historical Society uses its Bancroft income to award annually one individual, museum, historical association, genealogical society, school project, or committee in the state that has advanced the cause of education, awareness, and preservation of Colorado history.

Sandra Dallas has pointed out, "Anybody who cares about history is indebted to Caroline for saving stories and recollections of the old timers she interviewed." Coloradans are also indebted to Caroline for her magnanimous money gifts to support and advance the understanding of our past. David Halaas praises his old friend as a "useful, possibly praiseworthy, presenter of myths about the West. I am comfortable with myths," he says, "if they bring knowledge of the West."

No matter how often contemporary historians might condemn Caroline's embroidered stories of the past, the love of a mythic West remains constant among readers. Caroline targeted an audience that was hungry for romance and built a career upon it. Documented, foot-noted history for a different readership fills library and bookstore shelves. It's a matter of choice.

Notes

1. Frances Melrose, "State's unsinkable Miss Bancroft writes on," *Rocky Mountain News*, August 8, 1977.
2. Robert Irving Woodward, *Saint John's Church in the Wilderness: A History of St. John's Cathedral in Denver, Colorado, 1860–2000*, Prairie Pub., 2001.
3. Frances Melrose, "State's unsinkable Miss Bancroft writes on," *Rocky Mountain News*, August 8, 1977.
4. Ed Quillen, "Roundup," *Denver Post*, 2000.
5. Marilyn Griggs, "Caroline Bancroft, Portrait of a Popular Historian," *Where* Magazine, July 1974.
6. Frances Melrose, "State's unsinkable Miss Bancroft writes on," *Rocky Mountain News*, August 8, 1977.
7. Caroline Bancroft Papers, Box 15, Western History Department.
8. Marilyn Griggs, "Caroline Bancroft, Portrait of a Popular Historian," *Where* magazine, July 1974.
9. Caroline Bancroft Papers, Box 24, Western History Department, Denver Public Library.
10. Marilyn Griggs, "Caroline Bancroft, Portrait of a Popular Historian," *Where* magazine, July 1974.

11. Frances Melrose, "State's unsinkable Miss Bancroft writes on," *Rocky Mountain News*, August 8, 1977.

12. Diploma, Caroline Bancroft Papers, Western History Department, Denver Public Library.

13. Tom Noel, Editor, *The Glory That Was Gold*, Published by Central City Opera House Association Guild, 1992.

14. Caroline Bancroft Papers, Western History Department, Denver Public Library.

15. Randy Welch, "Old Money Meets New Money," *Colorado Homes & Lifestyles*, January–February 1984.

16. Caroline Bancroft Papers, Western History Department, Denver Public Library.

17. Frances Melrose, "How Fred Mazzulla Collected The West," Denver Westerners *Roundup*, June, 1975.

18. Olga Curtis, "The Battling Historians," *Empire* magazine, the *Denver Post*, January 16, 1972.

19. Interview of Mollie Lee Beresford by Marilyn Griggs Riley, January 2002.

20. Interview of Liston E. Leyendecker by Marilyn Griggs Riley, 2000.

21. Alfred E. Johnson Correspondence, Western History Department, Denver Public Library.

22. Kristen Iversen, *Molly Brown: Unraveling the Myth*, Johnson Books, 1999.

She Won Colorado's First Pulitzer Prize

Mary Coyle Chase
(1906–1981)

Mary and her springer spaniel friend share a chintz-covered sofa in her Circle Drive Denver home, "The house," Mary said, "that Harvey bought." (Western History Department, Denver Public Library)

In 1923, sixteen-year-old Mary Coyle wore a black velvet hat and lace dress when she applied for a summer job at the *Rocky Mountain News* in downtown Denver. The newspaper hired her. Twenty-two years later, Mary Coyle Chase, married and the mother of three young sons, won the 1945 Pulitzer Prize in drama for her three-act comedy, *Harvey*. She was the first Coloradan to win the coveted annual prize.

Harvey was a smash hit on Broadway, and Mary was rich nearly overnight. That was a shock to the attractive woman who had always thought of money as something you owed, not owned. After *Harvey*, life was never the same for Mary and her husband, Bob, whose own career at the *Rocky Mountain News* began as a reporter, advancing to city editor and then associate editor. Winnings from the Pulitzer and the avalanche of profits from the play were definitely welcomed in the Chase home. The bonanza increased the family income from $55 to $1,800 per week in a matter of forty-eight hours. More money followed when Universal Studios bought the film rights for $1 million, at that time the most ever paid for motion picture rights, with Jimmy Stewart starring as Elwood P. Dowd in the Hollywood version. *Harvey* had grossed $9 million by 1951 and continues to earn royalties. Translated into many foreign languages, the comedy played in theaters all over the world. "The only ones who didn't understand it were the French," Mary observed.[1]

Harvey is about a six-foot, one-and-one-half-inch-tall rabbit who is invisible most of the time to everyone but an amiable alcoholic Denver bachelor, Elwood P. Dowd. He meets Harvey, who is leaning against a lamppost, one night on Denver's Fairfax Street between East Eighteenth and Nineteenth Avenues. Harvey and Dowd log considerable time at Charlie's Bar. Veteran vaudeville comedian Frank Fay played the role of Dowd when *Harvey* opened at the Forty-Eighth Street Theatre in New York City on November 1, 1944, during World War II. The enduring and poignant comedy ran for 1,775 performances, one of the longest-running plays in theater history. *Harvey* makes a strong case for the importance of free spirit, generosity, and imagination—personal qualities that Mary despaired of ever recapturing after winning journalism's gold ring.[2]

Harvey's phenomenal success ended the Chase family's privacy. Photographers and interviewers came to their door and the doorbell rang. Then the "wrecking crews," as Mary labeled them, arrived. "The first wrecking crew refuses to believe you wrote the play—but let your cousin in Leavenworth [Penitentiary] use your name on his play. Another crew discusses you with others: 'That dame! When I first knew her she was eating canned soup without taking off the tin, and her feet don't track.'" Then she lamented, "There are always the salesmen and salesladies. I have stood in fitting rooms knee deep in costumes designed for Dracula: 'That's stunning on you, dear. We thought of you when that came in.'"[3] Brock Pemberton, who produced the Broadway *Harvey*, observed that "a hit is always a traumatic thing for playwrights: Most follow the whiskey-and-soda route, but a few are smart enough to go back to work. Mary did both for a time and then stopped drinking entirely."[4] Her story, however, began long before *Harvey*.

In Mary's youth, Denver was a small town. "Downtown was a lot of little low buildings, and you could number the good restaurants on one hand. It's an interesting town, controlled by about six families. They don't want any industry here, but I love Denver."[5] Mary was born in 1906 at 532 West Fourth Avenue, a home on the wrong side of Capitol Hill where wealthy Denverites like the "six families" lived. Her father, Frank Coyle, a salesman for a flour mill, had paid $2,500 for a small house near the South Platte Valley industrial area. During childhood, Mary and her three older brothers wore clothing carefully sewn by their mother, Mary McDonough Coyle, who had come from Ireland to Denver when she was sixteen.[6]

The Coyles' humble home was crowded with four other family members: Uncles Peter, Timothy, James, and John McDonough, all born in Ulster. They entertained the Coyle children with Irish tales of pookas, large, mythical animals much like Harvey. Mary's mother told her children about Irish fairies—banshees, cluricaunes, and leprechauns, advising Mary to "never make fun of those whom others consider crazy, for they often have a wisdom of their own. We pay them a great deal of respect in the old country, and we call them fairy people."[7]

Irish myths and superstitions were as much a part of the children's diet as their breakfast oatmeal. Kira Roark, goddaughter of Peggy and

133

Wallis Reef, remembered that Mary, was "extremely superstitious and although it often appeared to be an act, she really did believe in such things as reading tea leaves and fortune-telling." Mary's slightly off-beat view of the world was anchored in family stories about spirits and Celtic mysticism.

The Coyle household needed all the money it could get. Adult clothing came from bargain basements, and Mary's handmade underwear occasionally revealed the flour mill legend, "Pride of the Rockies," as she swung on the school playground's climbing bars. She was a vigorous, confident child and pretty, too, with deep brown hair, pale white skin, and large blue eyes.

As a young girl, Mary showed an affinity for the written word. She walked regularly to the neighborhood library and at age eight read Charles Dickens's *Tale of Two Cities*. At ten she read the essays of nineteenth-century British author Thomas De Quincey because she was enchanted by his last name, which she saw on a library bookshelf. At eleven, Mary began skipping school to walk the many blocks to downtown Denver's thriving theater district. Her first theater experience, paid for with a dollar she had been given, was at the Denham Theater. "A big crowd was going in for the matinee. I'd never been to a play, the admission was $1, and so I went in. The play was *Macbeth*." Another favorite was *The Merchant of Venice*. William Shakespeare's plays had her hooked on the theater. She read all she could about plays and playwriting and saw everything she could. "I got the highest grades for studies and the lowest for deportment," Mary recalled of her elementary school days. Historian Caroline Bancroft said her friend would be the first to tell that she came from one of the rowdiest gangs on the west side. "I had a reputation for physical daring and some notoriety for getting other children into mischief," Mary said.[8]

Reading and studying served her well. After graduation at age fifteen from the first West High School, at West Fifth Avenue and Fox Street, she entered the University of Denver. Although money was scarce in the Coyle household, her mother had saved for years, and some of the money paid for Mary's tuition. She studied the classics for two years, reading them in their original languages. In 1923, dressed in black lace, she charmed the city editor of the *Rocky Mountain News* into giving her a summer job.[9] Her "wages" consisted of carfare. "I wanted a job on a newspaper so I could study people, meet life, and later put it into plays. I wanted to see how people reacted under stress, how they spoke in time of crisis," Mary said. By this time she was a beautiful woman with a flawless complexion and luxuriant brown hair swept back from her face.

She transferred to the University of Colorado in Boulder, where she failed to be invited to join a sorority, a painful rejection that was never quite erased. Later, Mary used this disappointment for one of her first plays, *Sorority House*, in which an unsophisticated college coed triumphs over condescending peers. The three-act comedy was first produced in Denver in 1939 and then became a moderately successful movie. She left college after her junior year and returned to the *News* in 1925 as a full-time reporter, this time at a salary of $15 per week.

Sober, objective newspaper reporting was practiced, but the turbulent 1920s were dominated by the colorful journalistic styles of *Denver Post* reporters like Damon Runyan and Gene Fowler. Newspapers were recording Charles Lindbergh's transoceanic flight, the Dempsey-Tunney prizefight, Prohibition, local stories of organized crime, gang killings, the Ku Klux Klan, illicit love nests, sentimental tributes to mothers, and heartbreaking lost-dog stories. Reporters worked long hours, drank hard at the Denver Press Club, and stopped at nothing to beat the competition to a good story.

Circulation wars among the city's newspapers resulted in "extra" editions that raised circulation totals and increased profits. Harry Rhoads, a photojournalist for sixty-nine years, often worked twenty-four-hour shifts at the *News* and was on call seven days a week to shoot spectacular pictures of the best and worst in human behavior. Presses ran at night to print extras, and newsboys ran through dark streets shouting headlines, wakening sleeping citizens.[10] The *News* had a siren on its roof and the *Denver Post* had a big bell. "The bell tolled and the siren's tail was twisted whenever circulation gains were scored," wrote Robert L. Perkin in *The First One Hundred Years: An Informal History of Denver and the* Rocky Mountain News. The advent of the first Denver radio stations, KLZ in 1921 and KOA in 1924, plus a negotiated peace between the two major papers, mostly ended the practice of extra editions.

Mary, age eighteen, flourished in the exciting and rowdy world of Denver journalism. She dressed in the flapper style of the period—

Playwright Mary Chase and Harry Rhoads are clowning at a Denver Press Club event in the early 1940's. (Western History Department, Denver Public Library)

short skirt and bobbed hair—and was a curious, aggressive reporter. A rumor had circulated at the *News* that she was hired because "she combined an exquisite profile with very nice legs. We of the staff agreed," wrote *News* columnist Lee Casey, "but we also agreed that a comely body housed a most unusual mind." She quickly adopted the bland boldness of a good cityside reporter. "She would perch on the rim of the copy desk," wrote fellow reporter Reef, "and give translations of unusual Latin authors, and after the paper had gone to press, would sit around the office and drink quick ones with the fellows on the late trick."[11] The legendary Rhoads, an authority on feminine beauty, said, "Mary was the most beautiful newspaperwoman ever to work in Denver."[12]

Pretty or not, she covered tragedy and action and also served for a short time as society editor, which provided some of the comic observations that later appeared in her plays. *News* columnist Lee Casey wrote in 1945:

They tell many stories about Mary Coyle, some true. She was the first nonmale reporter to cover the fights at the Denver Athletic Club. Amateur fights are frequently gory, and Mary fainted when one fighter seemed to be coming apart. When she recovered, she kept right on her job and her account made the front page.

The Mary of those days was insubordinate, impatient of authority, perfectly willing to make and abide by her own rules. Her hours, too, were largely of her own choosing. The editors did curse, but after her copy appeared in print, the readers called for more.

Mary Coyle was soon well-known in Colorado for daredevil reporting: she became the newspaper's "stunt girl" on stories, a competitive reporter determined to get a story at any cost and before anyone else. Although she was superstitious, she violated one of the strongest superstitions of hard-rock miners. In 1927 they were tunneling from both entrances to complete the Moffat Tunnel under the Continental Divide and believed it was bad luck to allow a woman in the tunnel while they were working. Mary talked a male reporter into lending her an extra pair of trousers and a miner's cap. She went inside the tunnel disguised as a man and was there for the final hole-through. After the final blast had ripped away the last core of rock separating the two entrances, she stumbled through smoke, fumes, and broken granite and shook the hand of another *News* reporter who had come in from the other side. She got the story and nothing happened to the mine.[13]

Mary's carefree determination to get a good story involved a near disaster on a mining explosion assignment. She and Reef were flying over the mountains in a worn-out, single-engine plane piloted by Cloyd Cleavenger, who had once been a partner of Charles Lindbergh. The plane's engine made a terrible noise, died, and all was silence. Mary, who was growing hoarse trying to shout to Reef over the engine's roar, told the terrified Reef, "That's better. Now we can talk without all that noise." Cleavenger flipped the plane into two screaming dives, the motor caught, "and life for Mary and me went on. She thought it was great fun," said Reef. The pilot's story of the plane trip, with photographs of both *News* reporters, received as much space as the story of the mining explosion.[14]

"In the 1920's," wrote newspaperman Bob Chase, Mary's husband, "a reporter had a front row seat to life."[15] In the course of one day, Mary motored around Denver with photographer Rhoads driving either his Model T or his motorcycle. They could begin at the Police Court, attend a murder trial at the West Side Court, cover a society party at Mrs. Crawford Hill's mansion at 969 Sherman Street, and rush to a shooting at 11 P.M. One night a family reunion spiked with Prohibition liquor ended in a brawl with three dead and three left. Mary loved the dignified aplomb of one survivor: "When the man opened the door to see Rhoads and me, he said, 'Go away. I've talked it over with the folks, and we've decided not to put anything in the papers about this.'"[16]

News reporter Maurice "Spider" Leckenby, later newspaper publisher in Steamboat Springs, Colorado, wrote that "Mary was a good reporter. She had energy and lots of savvy. She could get news and chase pictures."[17] Once, to illustrate a sensational society divorce story, the city editor wanted a photo of the man in the case. There was no picture in the newspaper morgue and reporters were turned down at the family home. Then Mary remembered having seen a photo of the man with a tennis team on a wall at the Denver Country Club. She took a bus to the club, boldly walked in, and took the picture off the wall. Just as she had it, the club manager received a telephone call warning about the picture. Mary ran out into the street, flagged down a truck, and ordered the driver to "drive me to the *Rocky Mountain News* as fast as you can." The trucker obeyed and took her to the newspaper's offices, while Mary clung to the running board. When she arrived, she dashed upstairs and handed the photo to Rhoads, who copied it quickly and gave it back to her. As the country club manager came panting up the stairs, Mary handed the picture to him and asked innocently, "Is this what you're looking for?"[18]

Mary reveled in the center of the action, the newsroom, where reporters often played practical jokes on one another while waiting for assignments. She played one on the city editor at a particularly hectic time just before Christmas. The *News* and the Good Fellows Club had cosponsored a Christmas basket distribution to the poor, and Mary called Eddie Day, the city editor, just at deadline time when he would be the most frantic. An excellent mimic, Mary, shifting into her mother's Irish brogue, disguised her voice. "There wasn't no turkey like your paper said," she shrieked, "nothing but one measly sausage and some wormy apples!" She whined that it was "a cryin' shame that anyone in the name of Christian charity would give poor children rotten apples." She labored the point for several minutes. Day couldn't stop her tirade. Mary finally hung up, only to call him again in ten minutes to complain about "them wormy apples." Other reporters joined in the fun, until the apoplectic editor stopped answering the phone. Later, when he learned that Mary was the source of the Christmas basket prank, Day fired her. "But it didn't last long," she gaily said. "They asked me to come back, and I did."[19]

Mary and her good friends shared membership in the Denver Woman's Press Club: *News* reporters Helen Marie Black, who later managed the Denver Symphony Orchestra; Greta Hilb; and society editor Margaret Harvey. One of her best friends, whom Mary nicknamed "Collie," was nonmember Caroline Bancroft, who wrote for the *Post* and later appointed herself the grande dame of Colorado history. "Both of us were outspoken and full of shenanigans," recalled Bancroft.

In 1934, Mary and Caroline gave a party for visiting poet, *New Yorker* writer, and Algonquin Round Table wit, Dorothy Parker, who was famous for her quip that "Men never make passes/At girls who wear glasses." According to Caroline, who had known Parker for years, Parker told them that she wanted to meet "real people, not stuffed shirts." Obliging their famous friend's request, Mary and Caroline invited bootlegger Ed Rossi; local prizefighter Eddie Mack, and colorful high society leader Louise Hill (Mrs. Crawford), who furnished the liquor, pimps, and madams to a vacant house near East Eleventh Avenue and Ogden Street for a small party of twenty guests. Instead hundreds came, including Old Guard society members, Colorado governor and Mrs. Edward C. Johnson, and other civic leaders. Mary and Caroline discovered that Jack Carberry and three other *Post* reporters had sent bogus invitations to several hundred "stuffed shirts" as a prank on Parker and her friends. As people began arriving, traffic on Ogden and nearby streets clogged the neighborhood; the police ended both the traffic jam and the party.[20] Parker relished the evening and observed that Mary was "the greatest unacclaimed wit in America."[21]

Jeanett Letts, a reporter whose desk was next to Mary's at the *News*, remembered the moment that her colleague fell in love. Mary looked up as tall, handsome Robert L. Chase came through the door on his first day as a reporter at the *News*. She nudged Letts and said, "I'm going to marry that fellow." Letts owned her own car and lent it to Mary every night, who would offer to take Chase home. Bob, a lanky, dark-haired man, had as much serenity as Mary had vivacity; he was analytical while she was impulsive and unpredictable. They were married in 1928, and it was a happy marriage. His career at the *News* was distinguished, and he was regarded as "one of the most respected news men in the Rocky Mountain Empire," according to Margaret Harvey.

"Before I left the *News*, after a total of seven years, I had seen a lot," Mary said. She had gone to the County Hospital to get a feature story "about an old Chinese man dying broke so far away from his native land." There she saw cot after cot of the penniless aged dying alone and forgotten. "In a flash, I made an estimate of it all—the way youth does. What had meaning? What mattered?" Mary concluded that there were only three things worth bothering about: love, laughter, and beauty.[22] She had watched the way Mrs. Crawford (Louise) Hill greeted guests in her mansion. "I had seen the tight composure on the faces of defendants in murder trials as the jury entered with a verdict. I had been impressed with the way District Attorney Philip S. Van Cise walked like a Shakespearean actor. I had fixed many conversations, many phrases in my mind. I had learned the pacing of words, where to fix the eye, and incline the ear."[23]

The *News* wanted her to stay, but Mary, who had "married the boss" and was unconcerned about being jobless, quit in 1931 and began doing all the things she wanted to do. She bore three children: Michael in 1932, Colin in 1935, and Barry in 1936. She read plays, wrote a weekly radio program for the Teamsters' Union, and worked part-time in public relations to help pay the bills. Wearing a large picture hat, high heels, large earrings, and a dress "best described as slinky," she often joined the strikers' lines. A champion of the underdog, particularly Spanish Americans, Mary served coffee and sandwiches to the picketers and bullied police to let them continue.[24]

A newspaperman's salary was comparatively small for a family of five, and bill collectors frequently visited the Chase home. "I wasn't a very good businesswoman," Mary sighed. "Whenever I had to go to the Denver National Bank to ask for a loan, I always bought a new hat on credit so I wouldn't look tacky when I walked in. Since it was often a fifty-dollar hat, I was sunk before I started." Whenever she was lonely, Mary said, she would invariably get a letter from the bank that would cheer her immensely. The salutation "Dear Madam" would sound warmhearted, and the text concerning money she had borrowed for household and hospital bills would have an intimate touch.[25] Once, optimistically expecting a check that failed to materialize, she spent $200 for portraits of her sons. It took nearly two years to pay off the photographer. "On the fifth of each month, the photographer's secretary phoned to remind me of the payment," said Mary, "and we had many a long chat. When I finally got the debt paid off, the secretary called me as usual. She said, 'Mrs. Chase, we've discussed so many things in the past months, I kind of feel as if you're a friend. So, I just called to say I miss you.'" Touched, Mary sent her $1.50 to buy herself a couple of drinks.[26]

The family's chronic lack of cash did not interfere with their living well. Mary's emotional swings between gaiety and melancholy were balanced by her husband's steady nature. Both took great pride in their children, their extended families, and their friends—labor organizers, Junior League charity workers, grocery boys, bankers, teachers, and always, newspaper people. Friends would come by for a drink and frequently stay for dinner prepared by Mary, who was an indifferent cook. She tripled recipes to save time. Newsman Gene Cervi and his wife visited the Chases often for the conversation and the laughter, not for the food. At dinner one night, Cervi complimented Mary on the dessert, very sweet lemon meringue pie in a graham cracker crust. Bob interrupted Cervi: "Don't tell her it's good, or we'll have it for the next two weeks."[27]

"Mary did not have an organized mind," said her Denver Civic Theater friend, Mollie Lee Beresford. "She was so funny and could turn anything into a joke. But orderliness did not appeal to her. When my husband Howard and I went to her house, there were dishes in the sink, dirty ash trays, dogs. After *Harvey*, she asked Lolita Powell and me to visit her new Circle Drive house. The tour included the kitchen, and Mary said to us, 'Well, there aren't any dishes in the sink. This is what money can buy!'"[28]

In the early 1930s the Chase family was living in a small bungalow at 1364 Saint Paul Street in east Denver, and Mary had begun writing plays in her dining room. "From the beginning, she had trouble getting her characters on and off the stage, so she hit upon the device of using spools as members of the cast. She'd lay out a miniature stage area beside her typewriter, then pencil each character's name on a spool top. That way, she always knew who was still in front of the footlights, not doing anything to carry the play forward, and she'd be reminded to give him an exit line."[29]

Despite the quick writing habits Mary had developed as a reporter, writing plays took much more time and labor. Her first play, *Me Third*, was completed about the time her third son, Barry, was born. *Me Third*, renamed *Now You've Done It*, was the rowdy tale of a political candidate and the ex-cashier of a bordello. It was presented in 1937 by the Work Projects Administration (WPA) at the old Baker Theater at 1447 Lawrence Street. Denver critics liked it very much. Broadway producer Brock Pemberton bought the play, and five weeks after Barry's birth, Mary went to New York on her first trip east of Colorado. The play was a flop, running only seven weeks. Bob Chase advised his wife to get right back to her typewriter: "It's just like falling off a horse. You'll never write another play if you don't do it immediately."[30] Pemberton and the director, Denver-born Antoinette Perry, for whom the annual Tony Award for excellence in professional theater is named, also told her to continue writing. She did.

Like many of her plays, the next one, *Sorority House*, was based on her own experience, this one growing out of Mary's pain during rush week at the University of Colorado. Sensitive and proud, she had found it hard to grow up in a working-class neighborhood in a town like Denver, where the "Sacred 36" families were all-important. Mary's heroine is a poor girl snubbed in college, but who comes out on top. The comedy was a moderate success and later became a movie. However, "After years of study, I had had one failure on Broadway, one play done by the films, and two published. All I had to show for it were new slipcovers, and draperies, a Ford car, and monthly bulletins from the Dramatists Guild. My friends regarded my playwriting as harmless amusement."[31]

By 1941, Mary said, she had given up theater. "I had been kicked in the head by reviewers, and I realized I didn't have to try anymore. I stopped my subscription to *Variety* and said, 'Forget this.'"[32] But she could not forget writing. Her concentration at the typewriter remained unaffected by her husband, her children, or her ever-increasing number of friends.

The playwright, who appeared to be self-reliant, had a tendency to depend on mystical influences such as fortune-telling and dreams for writing ideas. For example, she once had a dream in which she saw a psychiatrist being followed by a large white rabbit. Mary had to figure out why, and it wasn't too difficult for a person who had grown up with Irish folklore and legends populated by pookas, poltergeists, and little people. Mary's offbeat logic supplied an answer that had been dormant in her mind for several years. Her answer was *Harvey*, a cheering play that won the Pulitzer Prize.

One winter morning in 1942, as World War II sobered the nation, Mary looked out her living room window and saw a sad-faced, middle-aged woman walking drearily up the street to the bus stop. "I was not acquainted with this woman, nor she with me. I am not to this day, but I had heard her story. She was a widow who had worked for years to send her only son through college. The day I looked at her, her boy had been dead about two months, killed in action in the Pacific. I asked myself a question: could I ever write anything that could make that woman laugh again?"[33] Her purpose in writing *Harvey* was indeed to make the widow laugh. "I didn't write any of the plays to make money. I wrote each one for a reason of my own. I'm convinced that if I'd written for money, it would have never come," Mary said.[34]

It took Mary two years to write the play that made her famous, working, as she put it, "in a trance. I'm only half here when I'm writing a play." During this time, her sons took full advantage of their mother's glassy-eyed condition. One day, in front of her blank stare, they carried out all the silver and buried it in the garden, where some unrecovered pieces might still be interred. The Chase boys quickly learned that when their mother was under the spell of playwriting, they could ask and get permission for things that ordinarily she would never allow. They hooted at her idea of an invisible rabbit who was exactly their father's height. They began ignoring her order to hang up their coats, because "Harvey will do it."[35] Their pranks rarely interrupted Mary's concentration. She worked with the radio blaring World War II news of Dunkirk through the casualties of Bastogne. In 1944, after she finished the play, originally titled *The White Rabbit*,

Mary Chase poses with Harvey, who made only one appearance in a preview performance and never appeared again. The audience had its own idea of what Harvey looked like and couldn't believe a man in a rabbit suit. (Rocky Mountain News)

Mary tried it out relentlessly on Civic Theater members, Wally and Peggy Reef, Gene Cervi, Caroline Bancroft, and even her cleaning woman, who listened to the play instead of cleaning. The play was sold, produced by Pemberton, directed by Perry, and then cast. Frank Fay, Josephine Hull, and Jane Van Duser played the principal roles.

During rehearsals for *Harvey*, Mary worried that the play would not succeed unless the rabbit actually appeared. She had insisted that the rabbit appear once after the second-act curtain, over the objections of the producer. "I bothered the director about it until she rented a $650 rabbit suit. At the preview, the rabbit made an entrance at the end of the second act. It was disastrous. He made only one crossing of the stage, and the play went out the window. People couldn't believe a man in a rabbit suit; they already had their own idea of what Harvey looked like."[36] The rabbit never appeared again.

Mary borrowed a dress from a Denver friend to wear to the opening night preview; her purse was empty except for a tube of bright red lipstick and a letter from her husband that read, "Don't be unhappy if the play does not succeed. You still have your husband and your three boys, and they all love you."

Harvey's principal visible character is Elwood P. Dowd, a wealthy, middle-aged alcoholic whose companion is a king-sized rabbit. Dowd finds Harvey leaning against a Denver lamppost one night after a round of Denver bars. Dowd's sister Veta and her daughter, Myrtle May, are living with him, and the women don't like the invisible Harvey. He spoils their social life because friends of the family tend to stay away after Dowd introduces them to Harvey or after finding Dowd reading to him. Dowd discusses the effect Harvey has on others:

> Harvey and I sit in the bars and we have a drink or two and play the jukebox. Soon the faces of the other people turn toward mine and smile. They are saying: "We don't know your name, Mister, but you're a lovely fellow." Harvey and I warm ourselves in all these golden moments. We have entered as strangers—soon we have friends. They come over. They sit with us. They tell us about the terrible things they have done. The big wonderful things they *will* do. Their hopes, their regrets, their loves, their hates. All very large because nobody ever brings anything small into a bar. Then I introduce them to Harvey. And he is bigger and grander than any-

thing they offer me. When they leave, they leave impressed. The same people never come back—but that's envy. There's a little bit of envy in the best of us. Too bad, isn't it?

In Act III the psychiatrist, Dr. Chumley, who is trying to help Dowd, prepares to give him a serum that will banish Harvey forever. Dowd is somewhat unstrung but agrees because Veta has arranged for the procedure—it will make her happy, and he has always wanted his sister to be happy. Before injecting the serum, Chumley asks Dowd how he met Harvey. Dowd replies:

> That was a rather interesting coincidence, Doctor. One evening several years ago I was walking early in the evening along Fairfax Street—between 18th and 19th … I heard a voice saying, "Good evening, Mr. Dowd." I turned and there was this great white rabbit leaning against a lamp-post. Well, I thought nothing of that, because when you have lived in a town as long as I have, you get used to the fact that everybody knows your name.
>
> Well, anyway, we stood there and talked, and finally I said— You have the advantage of me. You know my name and I don't know yours. Right back at me he said, "What name do you like?" Well, I didn't even have to think a minute. Harvey has always been my favorite name. So I said "Harvey," and this is the interesting part of the whole thing. He said—"What a coincidence! My name happens to be Harvey."[37]

After this session with Elwood, Dr. Chumley mutters to himself, "Fly specks. I've been spending my life among fly specks while miracles have been leaning on lamp-posts on 18th and Fairfax."

Also in Act III, Veta asks the cab driver to drive her and Dowd home after the medical procedure. The driver refuses because the patients are always changed afterward:

> On the way out here they sit back and enjoy the ride. They talk to me. Sometimes we stop and watch the sunsets and look at the birds flyin'. Sometimes we stop and watch the birds when there ain't no birds flyin' and look at the sunsets when it's rainin'. We have a swell time and I always get a big tip. But afterward,—oh—oh.

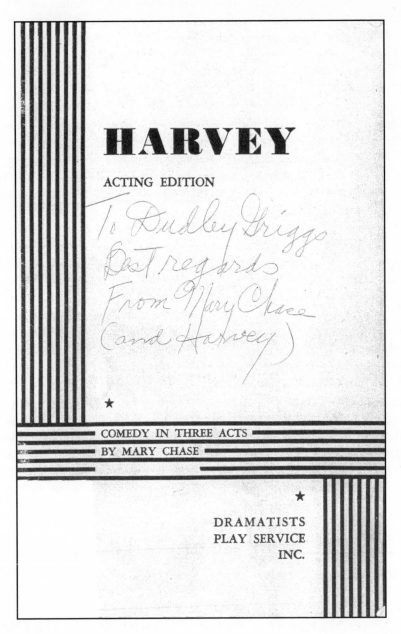

A signed copy of the original screenplay of Harvey.

They crab, crab, crab. They yell at me to watch the lights, watch the brakes, watch the intersections. They scream at me to hurry. They got no faith—in me or my buggy—yet it's the same cab—the same driver and we're goin' back over the very same road. It's no fun—and no tips.

Veta assures the cabbie that Dowd will tip him generously. "Not after this he won't. Lady, after this, he'll be a perfectly normal human being and you know what bastards they are!"[38]

"I will never forget Boston," Mary wrote of the pre-Broadway stagings. There she had heard comedian Frank Fay, playing the role of Elwood Dowd, say his opening line dozens of times. "Hello," he said into the telephone, "you have the wrong number, but how are you anyway?" Dozens of times she had heard audiences laugh warmly at the clue to Dowd's offbeat character. For example, he buys two of the same magazine subscriptions from a solicitor, one for him and another for Harvey. "There lives the one and only critic in the whole world who saw what I was trying to do in *Harvey*. He is Leo Gaffney of the *Boston Record* who wrote, '*Harvey* is a play with a spiritual meaning in farce terms.' It is not a play about a drunk," she insisted, adding that "liquor was inserted to keep the play from being a sermon." Mary, however, acknowledged that alcohol gave her inspiration for *Harvey*.

Harvey officially opened November 1, 1944, at the Forty-eighth Street Theatre in New York City. Bob Chase had come for the opening, where he and Mary were astonished at the crowds. The superstitious Denver playwright had three tangible reasons to be optimistic about her play: a member of the cast gave her a lucky two-dollar bill; Josephine Hull, who played Veta, gave her a four-leaf clover; and a truck driver drove slowly next to the curb outside the theater and said to her, "Hello, Love." The driver "wasn't trying to pick me up," Mary explained. "That third sign was a benediction." *Harvey* was a solid smash, meaning it was difficult to buy tickets. Mary's good-luck signs were confirmed when veteran actor Frank Fay told her the next morning, "Kid, you have got a hit." When Mary asked if he was sure, Fay said, "You are a dumb Denver housewife," a remark that made them fast friends.[39]

There was a long line at the box office on November 2, and Mary and Bob looked at each other. "What now?" they asked. Theater people told them to celebrate, to do anything they wanted. But Mary's agent, Harold Freedman, told the couple to try to pretend nothing had happened. "Not knowing in the least what Freed meant, we decided to go on with our lives as usual, the same old ones," she said. The Chases took a train back to Denver the next day rather than joining the Broadway playgoing crowd. But the old life they had returned to was not there, a realization they were slow to comprehend.[40]

Mary had become a Denver celebrity. Walking down the street, she saw people whispering and staring at her. Many of the Denver society people who had snubbed her in her reporting days now showered her with attention. Photographers and interviewers came to her home. Storekeepers tried to sell her things that nobody else would buy. Old friends hesitated to call for fear of interrupting her. "I became deeply unhappy and suspicious of everyone. A poison took possession of me, a kind of soul sickness," she realized. Success didn't bring her peace of mind. Instead, she said, it "plowed up my contentment. I was afraid for awhile that I had shot everything with *Harvey*. I smoke, I

Mary Chase and Rocky Mountain News columnist Vince Dwyer (photo by James Hartley, 1974)

have a passion for big hats, I drink. Can you imagine anything more foul than to have written *Harvey* and being a teetotaler?"[41]

Recalling those turbulent years of learning how to live in harmony with fame and fortune, Mary wrote, "Most people believe that in this world there is a magic room, papered with money, lit with fame, resounding with the sweetest music of all, piped from heaven." Those same people, she said, "wonder how you got in there while they're kept out. Most people believe this as a fact and yet call a 6-foot white rabbit a fantasy."[42] "The things you see by the flares of sudden fame are shattering and terrifying. The glittering eye of Greed, the distorted faces of her sisters, Envy and Malice. These witches always come to the feast. They chill your heart and leave you alone in the world. But there are solid things that restore your faith—family and real friends and the spiritual truths—till finally you can conclude again that man is truly a magnificent creature, badly dressed sometimes."[43] For several years Mary lived in what she called "the failure of success," suffering from a serious depression that distractions helped to ease. A play she had written before *Harvey*, a tragedy entitled *The Next Half Hour*, was produced on Broadway in 1945 and closed in failure within a week.

In 1946 the Chases paid $35,000 for a mini-baronial house at 505 Circle Drive, "The House That Harvey Bought," in Denver's elegant Country Club neighborhood. It was built by philanthropist Mrs. Verner Z. Reed for her sister, Florence Titus. Mrs. Reed then built her own Tudor castle next door at 475 Circle Drive, one of Colorado's grandest mansions. Both homes were designed by Denver architect Henry Manning and built during the Depression to employ out-of-work artisans and craftsmen. Mary furnished the interior of their home with antique furniture, oriental rugs, and rare silver pieces. Although the new house was large and expensively decorated, the family dog usually occupied the best chair in the living room. The gardens reflected the playful Mary: a Chinese gazebo; cherub, frog, and dolphin statuary; fountains; and a large, hammered copper rendering of Pan, Greek god of the forests and mischief. Wild strawberries served as groundcover.

Three years after *Harvey* opened on Broadway, it came to Colorado and made Mary the state's favorite daughter. Her play was presented in the summer of 1947 at the Central City Opera House for thirty-three performances with the original cast. It returned to Central City in 1971 for a month of performances. The comedy played in Denver many times, at the Elitch Summer Theater, the Auditorium Theater, and the Bonfils Theater. The University of Denver awarded Mary an honorary Doctor of Letters for *Harvey* and she taught a course in playwriting at her old college that fall. Joe E. Brown, who also played the role of Elwood Dowd, performed the role more than 2,000 times in New York City, Denver, and dozens of other cities. Jimmy Stewart appeared in the part briefly on Broadway, then starred in the 1950 film.

Mary had written *Harvey* to allay the sadness of a grieving mother, and *Harvey* eventually allayed her own as well. She began commuting from Denver to New York and Europe, where different casts were performing in the play. "I would stand in the back and listen to the music of the audience laughing. I could stand, anonymous as a ghost in the lobby between acts, and see the smiling faces of people I would never know, enjoying the play. One night I heard a man say to a friend, 'The first time Mother laughed since Joe was killed.'"[44] Mary believed she had kept her 1942 bargain with the grieving woman at the bus stop.

Her old sense of humor gradually returned. Once, when she and Bob were staying at the Mark Hopkins Hotel in San Francisco before leaving on a trip around the world, she wrote their son a postcard: "Michael, dearest, do you remember when you were a little boy crying because you didn't have bikes and toys like your friends had? Your father and I told you we were saving for your future. Well, son, we were lying. Love, Mom."[45]

Mary returned to work and by 1951 had written a new, vividly imaginative play, *Mrs. McThing*. "Work is the solution; it stays with you when all else is gone," she said. She determined to write a play for an audience who could in no way hurt her; it was to be for children only. She refused to allow her agent, Harold Freedman, to present it to adult audiences, but he persuaded her to agree to a brief, two-week Broadway production. The comedy, starring Helen Hayes and nine-year-old Brandon De Wilde, opened in February 1952. The "play for children of all ages," a story about a snobbish woman, a witch, and a mob of gangsters, was a surprise hit. The fantasy examines the relationships between parents and children and connects with

Denver's Party Line

Pictured at one of the many parties for the cast of Mrs. McThing, were Mary Chase, author of the whimsical play, Helen Hayes, starring in the lead role, and Governor Thornton.
—*Rocky Mountain News* Photo by *Morris A. Engle.*

In 1952 Mary Chase, Broadway actress Helen Hayes, and Governor Dan Thornton attend a Central City Opera House Association party for the cast of Chase's whimsical comedy, Mrs. McThing, *starring Hayes. (Western History Department, Denver Public Library)*

theatergoers of all ages. In it, a nine-year-old boy is spirited away by a witch from his overly strict mother, played by Hayes, and is handed over to a gang of comic mobsters with whom he has a very good time at the Shantyland Pool Hall lunchroom. Hayes willingly undergoes the humbling experience of mopping the floors of the lunchroom in order to understand why her son prefers characters like Poison Eddie, Dirty Joe, and Stinker to her.

"I know plenty about the problems of parents," Mary said. "I have three sons. And now I have a 7-month-old granddaughter."[46] "A play is like a building," she explained. "One false line and the structure collapses. You can go so far by workmanship and technique, but from then on, the play's a hunch. It's like a party—it's good or bad, but you can't quite tell why." *Mrs. McThing* was a "good" play. It earned rave reviews and $2,000 a week in royalties, and ran on Broadway for one year, not two weeks.[47] In the summer of 1952, *Mrs. McThing* and its Broadway cast, including Helen Hayes, Irwin Corey, and Ernest Borgnine, came to the Central City Opera House for a four-week run. The play later became a film, starring Pat Boone, with its world premiere in Denver.

While *Mrs. McThing* was still on Broadway in the fall of 1952, another of Mary's plays, *Bernadine*, opened at the Playhouse Theater on Forty-Eighth Street, just off Broadway. *Bernadine* is about the half-real, half-fantasy world of teenage boys. Bernadine is an imaginary girl, a little beat-up and older than the seventeen-year-old boys, who knows only one word, *yes.* "I got the idea from watching my teen-age sons and their friends around the house, and I wrote the play about them and for them," Mary explained. As had happened with *Mrs. McThing*, the young audience she had expected was crowded out by enthusiastic adults, and again she began collecting $2,000 a week from the play's successful run.[48] Broadway theater fans began referring to Forty-Eighth Street as "Mary Chase Alley" because in 1952, a revival of *Harvey, Mrs. McThing*, and *Bernadine* were all playing on that street.[49]

By 1953, Mary, aged forty-six, with "the voluptuous figure of a real woman," a friend observed, lived a comparatively quiet life. She wore well-cut dresses in dark shades and one of her dozens of bright hats. Her life settled into a pleasant pattern that was a far cry from her pre-*Harvey* days. She would awaken at seven each morning, read several passages from the Bible, and go for a brisk forty-five-minute walk. "I got in the habit, walking the boys to school," she explained. Then she would work in her office until Bob came home from the *News*.

Whenever Mary announced that she was beginning a new play, her husband's only reaction was "Oh, God." She understood. "It's all been a little tough on Bob. When I married him, I was scatter-brained and willful; he had a reputation for integrity and endurance. He made it possible for me to write plays, and I hope *Harvey* has made up for unmended socks and bad meals. Bob grew prematurely gray, but he has been the Rock of Gibraltar. I have survived it, but it took all I had and then some. I had to borrow a little—from Bob and the Bible."[50]

Although she had been a loud and happy extrovert, Mary became reserved and quiet. When she went to New York City, she would stay only long enough to do any necessary rewriting of her scripts. "As soon as a play is launched," she said, "I immediately get on a plane to my family in Denver."[51]

Midgie Purvis, a 1961 fantasy-comedy starring Tallulah Bankhead that failed on Broadway, was Mary's final play. "I can't write for the theater now," she said. "There is no standard now. That's why we are having so many revivals instead of new shows on Broadway."[52]

Where Mary Coyle Chase had once been recklessly funny, after *Harvey* "mature thoughtfulness" replaced her enormous sense of fun. She helped friends through troubles, said her friend Margaret Perry. "In a way, she's a gentle bully about her friends' lives. She manages you into doing not what you *want* to do but what is *right* for you to do." Caroline Bancroft said, "If you're blue, she'll drop by your house to spend a whole afternoon hearing your troubles and cheering you up." Mary sent checks to needy friends, organized the House of Hope for female alcoholics, and joined the First Church of Christ, Scientist, at East Fourteenth Avenue and Logan Street. She stopped drinking alcohol. The only time Frank Fay, a recovering alcoholic, ever paid Mary a compliment was after she quit drinking. "He said, 'You're great, kid. Lots of bums can write a play, but when you get on the sauce and then get off, that takes doing,'" Mary recalled.[53]

"Mary Chase," said Caroline Bancroft, "had flair, cultivation, brains, and courage. After *Harvey*, Mary became more and more of a conformist. This town used to be full of characters and now few are left. She's still got an awful lot of individualism, an awful lot of courage, but she's not exuberant the way she used to be."[54]

In 1963, Mary donated the original manuscripts of *Harvey*, *Mrs. McThing*, and *Bernadine* to the University of Denver's Mary Reed Library for special use by students in the DU theater department. Copies of the two children's books she wrote, *Loretta Mason Potts*

Mary Coyle Chase's application for membership to the Denver Women's Press Club. (Western History Department, Denver Public Library)

and *The Wicked Pigeon Ladies*, are also available at the university. Mary didn't feel that book writing was her medium. The books she wrote "are written as a playwright would have handled it," she said.[55] She became an honorary member of the Denver Woman's Press Club and a board member of the Bonfils Theatre and the Denver Center for the Performing Arts.

In 1981, still a handsome woman with flashing blue eyes, Mary said, "I have no desire to write anymore. I have 11 grandchildren to enjoy," as well as the Chase mountain home near Elk Falls, Colorado. Looking back on a busy life, she had few regrets. "If I have any message at all for young writers it is this: Healing laughter is in order. A writer either weeps or praises. Look up and praise. The world has need of it."

Although her husband said, "I never thought someone like Mary could die," Mary Chase died of a heart attack in Denver on October 20, 1981, at age seventy-five. She was survived by Bob and their three sons, Michael and Berry of New York City and Colin of Toronto, Ontario. Bob died in 1990 at age eighty-five. The two are buried in

Crown Hill Cemetery, Michael Chase told a crowd at a ceremony at the Denver Center for the Performing Arts in 1999. He thanked the organization and its supporters for honoring his famous mother by inducting her into the center's Hall of Fame. Then he solemnly told the audience that his parents were buried next to Harvey.

"What a coincidence!" Elwood P. Dowd might well remark.

Gullible fans of Colorado's first Pulitzer Prize recipient might even visit the cemetery seeking a six-foot, one-and-a-half-inch stone rabbit obelisk. They won't find it. Bob and Mary lie in a plot deliberately chosen next to a Jefferson County couple that had died years earlier (1972 and 1987) named Harvey.

"Laughter heals," she believed. And Mary gets the last laugh.

Bob and Mary Chase are buried in a plot next to Harvey at Crown Hill Cemetery in Lakewood.

Notes

1. Frances Melrose, "Mrs. Chase pleased with care of 'Harvey,'" *Rocky Mountain News*, February 28, 1977.
2. Eleanor Harris, "Mary Chase, Success Almost Ruined Her," *Cosmopolitan*, February 1954.
3. Mary Chase, "My Life with Harvey," *McCall's*, February 1951.

4. Harris, "Mary Chase."

5. Ibid.

6. Frances Melrose, "Mrs. Chase pleased with care of 'Harvey,'" *Rocky Mountain News*, February 28, 1977.

7. John E. Drewry, ed., *More Post Biographies*, University of Georgia Press, 1947.

8. Frances Melrose, "Mrs. Chase pleased with care of 'Harvey,'" *Rocky Mountain News*, February 28, 1977.

9. Frances Melrose, "From Reporter to Pulitzer Prize Winner," *Rocky Mountain Memories*, Denver Publishing Company, 1986.

10. Morey Engle and Bernard Kelly, *Denver's Man with a Camera: The Photographs of Harry Rhoads*, Cordillera Press, 1989.

11. Drewry, *More Post Biographies*.

12. Frances Melrose, "Mary Chase: reporter to playwright," *Rocky Mountain News*, February 27, 1977.

13. Ibid.

14. Drewry, *More Post Biographies*.

15. Robert L. Chase, (no title, according to city editor now at *Rocky Mountain News*), *Rocky Mountain News*, April 22, 1984.

16. Mary Chase, "City Room to Stage," *Rocky Mountain News*, anniversary ed., April 19, 1959.

17. Maurice Leckenby, "Mary Cole Chase," *Colorado Editor*, vol. 33, 1958.

18. Frances Melrose, "Mary Chase: reporter to playwright," *Rocky Mountain News*, February 27, 1977.

19. Harris, "Mary Chase."

20. Caroline Bancroft, Oral History, Colorado Historical Society.

21. Mike Flanagan, "Mary Coyle Chase," *Out West*, *Denver Post*, November 14, 1981.

22. Mary Chase, "City Room to Stage," *Rocky Mountain News*, April 19, 1959.

23. Frances Melrose, "Mary Chase: reporter to playwright," *Rocky Mountain News*, February 27, 1977.

24. Drewry, *More Post Biographies*.

25. Harris, "Mary Chase."

26. Ibid.

27. Interview of Cle Cervi Symons by Marilyn Griggs Riley, 1999.

28. Interview of Mollie Lee Beresford by Marilyn Griggs Riley, 2000.

29. Bill Barker and Jackie Lewin, *Denver!*, Doubleday, 1972.

30. Jackie Campbell, "Writer Chase still enchants," *Rocky Mountain News*, April 17, 1981.

31. Mary Chase, "My Life with Harvey."
32. Jackie Campbell, "Writer Chase still enchants," *Rocky Mountain News*, April 17, 1981.
33. Chase, "My Life with Harvey."
34. Harris, "Mary Chase."
35. Ibid.
36. Ed Quillen, "Roundup," *Denver Post*, December 3, 1978.
37. *Harvey*, acting ed., Dramatists Play Service, 1943.
38. Ibid.
39. Harris, "Mary Chase."
40. Chase, "My Life with Harvey."
41. Ward Morehouse, "Mary Chase Finds 'Harvey' Has Changed Her Life," North American Newspaper Alliance, July 7, 1946.
42. Mike Flanagan, "Mary Cole Chase," *Out West*, *Denver Post*, November 14, 1981.
43. Hugh McGovern, "1945 Was Year for Mary Chase," *Rocky Mountain News*, January 23, 1951.
44. Mary Chase, "My Life with Harvey."
45. Michael Chase, speech, Colorado Performing Arts Hall of Fame, November 5, 1999.
46. Mark Barron, "Mary Chase Doesn't Act Part of Broadway Playwright," *Rocky Mountain News*, October 26, 1952.
47. Harris, "Mary Chase."
48. Ibid.
49. Mark Barron, "Mary Chase Doesn't Act Part of Broadway Playwright," *Rocky Mountain News*, October 26, 1952.
50. Chase, "My Life with Harvey."
51. Mark Barron, "Mary Chase Doesn't Act Part of Broadway Playwright," *Rocky Mountain News*, October 26, 1952.
52. Frances Melrose, "Mrs. Chase pleased with care of 'Harvey,'" *Rocky Mountain News*, February 28, 1977.
53. Ibid.
54. Caroline Bancroft, Oral History, Colorado Historical Society, 1977.
55. Marjorie Barrett, "Mary Chase's First Book Intriguing Children's Tale," *Rocky Mountain News*, September 24, 1958.

Suggested Reading

Abbott, Carl, Stephen J. Leonard, and Thomas J. Noel. *Colorado, A History of the Centennial State.* 4th edition. University Press of Colorado, 2005.

Athearn, Robert G., *The Coloradans,* University of New Mexico Press, 1976.

Gehres, Eleanor M., Sandra Dallas, Maxine Benson, and Stanley Cuba, eds. *The Colorado Book,* Fulcrum, 1993.

Lamar, Howard R. ed. *The New Encyclopedia of the American West,* Yale University Press, 1998.

Limerick, Patricia Nelson, *Something in the Soil: Field-Testing the New Western History.* W. W. Norton & Company, 2000.

Ubbelohde, Carl, Maxine Benson, and Duane A. Smith. *A Colorado History,* 8th ed. Pruett Publishing Company, 1976.

Compiled by Workers of the Federal Writers' Project of the Work Projects Administration in the State of Colorado, *The WPA Guide To 1930s Colorado,* University Press of Kansas, 1987.

Index

Marilyn Griggs Riley has lived in Park Hill, Denver, for most of her life. She graduated from East Denver High School and earned a BA in English literature from the University of Colorado, Boulder. She has an MA in mass communications from the University of Denver.

She taught middle school students in Jefferson County and Denver, but spent most of her twenty-five-year career at Denver's Manual High School where she taught literature, composition, and forensics. At Manual she learned about Justina Ford, MD, who became one of her topics.

For several summers Riley edited *Where* Magazine, a free weekly tourist publication promoting the city's restaurants, museums, and other places of interest to Denver visitors. Using the magazine's credentials, she met, interviewed, and wrote features stories about Caroline Bancroft, Helen Black, and Thomas Hornsby Ferril.

From 1975 until his death in 1988, Colorado Poet Laureate Ferril, author of six books of poetry and two volumes of essays, was a major presence in her life: lunches at the Ferril Table in the Denver Press Club, Thanksgiving dinners, and birthday parties with Tom, his wife Hellie, and guests who crowded their home where Tom taught the Downing Street Waltz to eight-year-old Anne Griggs. In 1981, Don Kinney, Channel Six television producer, and radio host/Rocky Mountain News columnist Gene Amole planned a half-hour television documentary about Ferril, who then suggested Riley write it. "Thomas Hornsby Ferril: One Mile Five-Foot Ten" was aired locally and nationally on the Public Broadcasting System. The documentary received an Emmy in 1981. Ferril asked the author to write the preface to his final book of poetry, *Anvil of Roses*.

Riley is a member of the Denver Woman's Press Club, the Denver Press Club, and the Monday Literary Club.